# SEASONS

## How to Develop Everlasting Faith in Uncertain Times

## SEASONS

*All Rights Reserved.*
Copyright © 2022 by Dr. Brenda Jefferson

No part of this book may be reproduced or transmitted in any form or by any means electronic or mechanical – including photocopying, recording, or by any information storage and retrieval system – without permission in writing from the publisher with the exception of quotes used in reviews. Please direct inquiries to: pkkid36@gmail.com

Scripture Music Group Publishing
805 E Bloomingdale Avenue
Valrico, FL. 33596

*Your support and respect for the property of this author is much appreciated.*

**NOTE:** All scriptures cited in this book are from the King James Version of the Bible, or the American Standard Version unless otherwise noted.

Library of Congress Control Number: 2022919761
ISBN: 978-1-73654465-5-0

*I would like to dedicate this book to those who have labored with me in the gospel during every season. I thank God for my husband, my children, my spiritual family, and the ministry. I am grateful for all of you, and I pray that this book is a blessing in your life.*

# Acknowledgments

God has truly given me wisdom and strength to endure every season. It is a blessing to serve in ministry and I appreciate all of your support.

To my husband, Bishop M.B. Jefferson, thank you for always being there to support me in everything that God has called me to do. I am grateful for your leadership and love.

To all of my children, both spiritual and natural, I pray that each of you would experience God in a supernatural way. Continue in the faith, no matter what trials and tribulations may come your way, always remain rooted and grounded in the Word of God.

# Table of Contents

Introduction ........................................................................ 2

Chapter One: Season In, Season Out ............................................ 6

Chapter Two: Jesus, Our Hope in Ages Past ............................... 30

Chapter Three: Trust in God - Understanding His Power .......... 60

30-Day Devotional ................................................................ 74

# Seasons

Dr. Brenda Jefferson

# Introduction

Jesus himself declared that the Kingdom of Heaven is like a tree. *'The Kingdom of Heaven is like unto a grain of mustard seed, which a man took, and sowed in his field: which indeed is the least of all seeds: but when it is grown, it is the greatest among herbs, and becometh a tree, so that the birds of the air come and lodge in the branches thereof,'* Matthew 13:31-32.

Often, life can seem cyclical. In our limited awareness, we can feel as though we are not progressing, or as if no visible growth is being made. However, during these seasons of maturation and development, we must trust the work that God is doing on the inside. We, as humans, are styled as trees (Psalms 1:2-3). *'She is a tree of life to them that lay hold upon her: and happy is every one that retaineth her. The Lord by wisdom hath foundeth the Earth and by understanding hath he established the Heavens,'* Proverbs 3:18-19.

All throughout scripture, we see references to nature, seasons, vines, and plants. Be it, the tree of knowledge in the first garden, or mention of a fig, olive, oak, palm, green bay, or cedar tree. We often hear the phrase, "the rose that grew from concrete." God empowers us through His Word. Be mindful that you can flourish during famine. You can bud, sprout, and grow in the middle of difficulty.

In Biblical terms, a tree can even symbolize long life, resiliency, being upright, new beginnings, and the gift of eternal life. These graceful, fragrant, and durable plants are useful and important throughout history, and throughout the world. In the middle of what you are going through, there may be reasons to mourn, but His presence also gives us reasons to celebrate. God's grace and wisdom supersedes the trials of the day, or the season that we may be in.

In His power, He can convict and comfort, command and empower, rule and rescue. The power of God is so resolute that it marches patiently, an enduring promise of hope. Through darkness, justice and mercy beckons us to walk on. The world around us groans in chaos, but in Jesus there is a tranquil peace that surpasses all understanding (Jeremiah 17:7-8). *You can make it!*

Every season serves a purpose. A tender prick of the heart during suffering allows us to press on another day. Keep your feet firmly planted in the House of God. The transformative process of the cross is one of rescue, reconciliation, restoration, recreation, and victory. If you are somewhere between what you know, how you feel, and what you see today – focus on His Word, obey God, and follow leadership as they follow Christ.

In seasons of discomfort, God is often leading you to the entrance of your next. May your life be a continual and pleasing sacrifice to God. Jesus died for you; He became your sin that you might become His righteousness. As believers in Christ, each of us must bear or produce *our own* fruit. As your old leaves and ways are pruned away, a brand-new change in thinking is being revealed. God is with you and His spirit is always leading and guiding you. There is breakthrough, healing, and deliverance found through the blood of Jesus. You can prosper and you can succeed. You can flourish and you can bloom. *'The righteous shall flourish like the palm tree: he shall grow like a cedar in Lebanon,'* Psalms 92:12.

Victory is a mindset, and you have to set your mind to be a winner. We pray that this book gives you the wisdom to march and not break rank, to persevere in the midst of hardship, to develop into your best self, and ultimately to become all that God desires you to be.

# Seasons

## CHAPTER ONE

## SEASON IN, SEASON OUT

"I am sick and tired of the pain this brings, John," Anita cried out in desperation. "There is so much to do and so little money!"

"Relax, Anita," John said, trying to comfort his wife. "This will pass."

It was the third month of living in their car bus and barely having enough to eat. Anita had been working three jobs and John had started taking evening home lessons for some kids who were being homeschooled. The time, truly, was very tough for the couple. Anita had been in and out of the hospital after battling an ectopic pregnancy that they eventually lost, and the cost of the necessary treatments ate into every bit of their savings. It was shortly after her dismissal from the hospital that the owner of the house where they lived asked them to leave because of how behind they were with rent.

"Will it ever get better?" Anita asked, tears welling up in her eyes. "I am so tired of all that is happening, and I feel so abandoned and left behind."

"But that is not true. You know that we have each other, and we would be able to scale through this, just like we always have."

John was equally tired of the current situation of his family. He wished he could provide everything that he and his wife needed, to leave the life they were living for good. He was heartbroken that he lost his first child with his wife and wished the situations were better to pacify their loss.

The couple prepared to go to retire for the night. They had a long day behind them, and yet another in front of them. Anita rushed to the bed and covered her head with the thin cloth they had as a duvet. The night was cold and as John looked back at his wife, he simply wanted it all to end. His mind traveled from pillar to coast, thinking of someone he could reach out to for help. He thought of his younger brother who had relocated to California a long time ago and was preparing to get married to the love of his life; he knew how hard it was to get in touch with him amidst his busy life as an architectural engineer. Then, he thought about his best friend in Dallas. It had been a long while since they last spoke and he did not think it would be okay to lay his burden on the chest of another man; for all he knows, they too could be going through their own challenges.

John laid down to sleep and closed his eyes. Before he slept off, he looked out the window of the bus at the sky and remembered all that his mother used to say to him when she was alive.

*'Son, if you give your burdens to God, He will be glad to take them and clear them out for your sake. Nothing lasts forever, you should know. Be grateful and live with a light heart always.'*

John closed his eyes firm for some seconds and mumbled some words to the invisible man in the sky. 'Lord, I do not know the plans that you have for me. It may not look good to me right now and I am tired of the state of my life and my family, but I choose to trust you. You have never forsaken me, and you would not start now." With that, he went to sleep, unbothered about the need to stay up thinking and very eager to start the new day.

"John!" Anita squealed, waking John up from the deep sleep he was in. He wiped his eyes, still squinted, with the back of his right hand. "John, wake up!"

"Is anything wrong?" John asked under his breath, still half asleep.

"Everything is right, John!" Anita said. "Everything!"

She handed John her mobile phone to see what it was that left her very excited. As John started to read, he sat up, paying more attention than ever.

"You got the job?!" John asked, jumping from the bed. He looked at his wife as she held her hands over her mouth and nodded. Turning back to the phone, he read the mail over and over again, saw the offer the company was ready to give, and saw that she could resume in the new month, that was less than two weeks away. It was a job she had applied for in the past but never got a response. The mail stated that her application had gotten lost in the mail, and they have seen that she was the best candidate for the role.

"This is God!" John said. He took his wife in his arms and squeezed her very tight, then fell on his knees and started to sing to God.

"Our tough times have passed!" Anita said, joining her husband to give thanks to God.

## Season In, Season Out.

*'To everything, there is a season, A time for every purpose under heaven: A time to be born, and a time to die; A time to plant, and a time to pluck what is planted; A time to kill, and a time to heal; A time to break down, and a time to build up; A time to weep, and a time to laugh; A time to mourn, and a time to dance; A time to cast away stones, and a time to gather stones; A time to embrace, and a time to refrain from embracing; A time to gain, and a time to lose; A time to keep, and a time to throw away; A time to tear, and a time to sew; A time to keep silence, and a time to speak; A time to love, and a time to hate; A time of war, and a time of peace,'* Ecclesiastes 3: 1-8.

The conversations we have as children of the Most High God, about the times and seasons in our lives may just not be enough. We may not have come to the reality of just how important we are to God and how much He wants only the best for us. Think back over your life. Have you ever gone into an airplane when you purchased a first-class ticket for a flight, and reflected on the service? Were you left by yourself to handle your luggage? Did you place your luggage in the same kind of overhead slots, as on the flight with a regular economy ticket? Did you have to hustle with your neighbor for a spot to place your arm, or did you have more than enough leg room? Did you have to eat regular snacks and 'plane food' or were you given the luxury of more and tastier options?

The difference is clear, for sure, and I can assure you that the treatment we are bound to receive from God is far better, and more 'expensive' than the most expensive first-class flight in the world. What is better? We do not get to pay!

Christians hardly soak themselves in the reality of who they are in Christ and what they are bound to enjoy because they have not returned to the Word of God to see for themselves, all that they have been promised. Now, if you have seen members of the army train or have intensive workouts, you may term it as suffering, pain, and even agony. They are made to go through tough procedures that will eventually prepare them to be a different version of themselves. A member who does not necessarily know what they are at the training school for, will look at the trainers with disgust a couple of times and agree that they are being maltreated. This pain and the training, it is the same with our God, and even with the life that we have been blessed with.

In life, we go through certain seasons and phases that are sure to make us doubt the hand of God, if we do not have our hearts grounded in the ways of our maker. I have seen people lose members of their families, I have seen marriages fail and partners crumble, and I have seen people lose opportunities and get laid off from work with no prior notice. It all happens, it is life. And I have also seen people get amazing job offers that they were not expecting, I have seen families receive life-changing opportunities, just like Anita and John in our little story back there, I have seen and experienced the birthing of very important things and one thing I can say for sure is this; seasons come, and seasons go.

Rain comes, and the people who do not understand the importance would talk about how much they hate the rain, and how they would rather spend the entire stretch of the season indoors. The sun comes, and those who prefer the calmness and coolness of the rainy season would rant about how hot it is and how they would do anything to live in a pool, or sleep on a waterbed. Seasons will come and seasons will go! The most important balance to all of them, is an understanding of the season that you are in.

To the farmer who has taken the time to observe the importance of both seasons, no one is more important than the other! Leviticus 26:4 says, *'then I will give you rain in its season, the land shall yield its produce, and the trees of the field shall yield their fruit.'* The important keyword in this verse is 'season.' If God gives us a thing when it is not the right season, then that thing will not be used in the way that it is supposed to be used. It is like handing a growing child the keys to a mansion that was purchased in his name. He or she has no good use for that house at the time, and rather than be a blessing (like it would be in the right season), it begins to look like a curse or burden for the child. Likewise, the blessing of the rain from God. The farmer has timed his planting, his waiting, and his harvest to get the most out of all the seasons, and there is probably not a better way to say, that every season you go through in life is meant for a reason. If the rain does not come, plants will not grow, if the rain lasts too long, plants will not grow, and if the sun lasts too long, plants will be parched, and they still will not grow.

Seasons will come and seasons will go. With everything, there is a cycle, or a period of time needed, for a certain purpose. Joy, pain, sunshine, and rain; you can't avoid these things. We all must go through our seasons. **In our lifetime, we will go through twenty-eight different seasons; they will make you or mar you, and that is up to how you handle it.** With each season comes challenges, and each season will affect your mood or attitude. Likewise, your attitude ultimately determines your altitude (how far you go). Always find the blessings in your trials, for trials bring blessings. Why? *'Wherein ye greatly rejoice, though now for a season, if need be, ye are in heaviness through manifold tempatations: that the trial of your faith, being much more precious than of gold that perisheth, though it be tried with fire, might be found unto praise and honour and glory at the appearing of Jesus Christ,'* 1 Peter 1:6-7.

The understanding of where a person is at in life is very important. When you recognize your current season, you are able to speak to God, hear from Him, and see the direction that He is leading you to go in, for maximum potential to be birthed.

The Bible says in Jeremiah 29:11, *'For I know the thoughts that I think toward you, says the LORD, thoughts of peace and not of evil, to give you a future and a hope.'* And in Jeremiah 1:5 it states, *'Before I formed you in the womb I knew you; before you were born I sanctified you; I ordained you a prophet to the nations.'* What do you see in these passages? I will tell you what I see.

Back to my reference of the first-class airplane, you do know that the flight attendants on the plane are aware that you will be present.

## Seasons

There is hardly ever a time where there would be no provision for any of your needs all through the flight, and that would not be possible if there were no prior plans and steps taken to prepare for your presence on the plane. So, because they have planned for you, they are able to take care of you completely. So, with these Bible verses, that is what I see; Complete care.

You were not created by chance, and you are not a burden to God. From the depth of His heart, He loves you and cares for you, and this is evident in the many things He has done for you and me until this day. If you are facing a certain downtime now, remember this and know that God has a plan for you even in that dark time. Maybe you had an experience that could have been completely avoided and it has led to deeper troubles than expected, so you think that was not in God's plan. You are wrong; God knows it all and He sees it all. Say this to yourself with a pat on the chest; whatever God has allowed; He will shine through.

The first few verses in Ecclesiastes 3, lets us know the different seasons and phases, that we are be bound to come face to face with in life. Tough times are not the end of our lives, and they are also not 'proof' that God is not present in our lives. Do not listen to that lie from the pits of hell. Listen, there are certain things that God needs to teach you that can never be taught in a place of comfort, and there are certain places you will need to get to in life - with their routes looking worse than a desert. Look at the lives of the children of Israel; their journey out of Egypt was not easy or smooth! The Bible says in Exodus 14:11-12, *'And they said unto Moses, Because there were no graves in Egypt, hast thou taken us away to die in the wilderness? Wherefore hast thou dealt thus with us, to carry us forth out of Egypt? Is not this the word that we did tell thee in Egypt, saying, Let us alone that we may serve the Egyptians? For it had been better for us to serve the Egyptians, than that we should die in the wilderness.'* For people who were kicked about and maltreated as slaves in Egypt, even the walk to their freedom seemed worse than their slavery and they wanted out! Yet, God had a plan for them, a place that they could call their home, but only if they would trust Him and walk through the season of hardship following His lead.

God is intentional about you. He makes no mistake, and as He sits in the Heavens, He knows and sees all that happens here on Earth. You are a child of God; He has your best interest in His heart, and He will always move mountains for you. For every time that you honor God with your trust and obedience, He will use your life as a means to show the world who He is, and what He can still do.

Enjoy every season of your life, knowing that it will pass. Yes, the good times will pass and so will the bad times, so you must understand how best to make use of it for the glory of God and for the uplifting of your spirit man.

**Trials and Tribulations experienced in seasons.**

*'And not only so, but we glory in tribulations also: knowing that tribulation worketh patience; and patience, experience; and experience, hope: And hope maketh not ashamed; because the love of God is shed abroad in our hearts by the Holy Ghost which is given unto us,'* Romans 5:3-5.

For instance, say a farmer has a couple of pepper seeds that he needs to grow in the space of three months. He wants to have an entire farm of growing pepper sin three months and he has all that he needs to make this a reality, in his hands. Now, he looks down at his seeds and says, 'no way in the world will I put these pretty little things down there in the soil!' and he proceeds to store the seeds up in his cupboard where they would be safe. In the next month, he surveys his garden and sees the same plain soil, sitting idle. He checks the jar of pepper seeds in his cupboard, and nothing has changed still. He still refuses to throw the 'precious' seeds into the soil. Lo and behold, the third month comes into fruition, and it is time for harvesting the expected peppers. What do you think he gets? Nothing.

The soil does not look like it is a pleasant place to be in, but who says that growth itself is a pleasant experience? Growth for anybody and anything is a gathering of lessons learned from certain experiences. There are countless instances in the Bible where people go through certain experiences and come out from them renewed.

In our lives, trials are very important to shape us into the form that is best for us, in our walk with Christ. Trials are not meant to break you, but to build you. They are not meant to break your spirit but to build your heart, to see things the way they are meant to be seen. Without these trials, you do not grow up, and you will be unable to move from where you are right now to where the Lord wants you to be in a few years. Trials are not always desirable, in fact, they are very far from it. This is so, because certain things need to be birthed in tough circumstances for them to stay.

We could look at the lives of some people in the Bible who went through very tough situations and came out of it victorious, just as God wants for you and me.

### 1. Job.

Growing up, I heard the story of the life of Job more times than I can count. Job had everything that a person could ever hope and wish for. Job 1:1-3 says *'There was a man in the land of Uz, whose name was Job; and that man was perfect and upright, and one that feared God, and eschewed evil. And there were born unto him seven sons and three daughters. His substance also was seven thousand sheep, and three thousand camels, and five hundred yoke of oxen, and five hundred [female donkeys], and a very great household; so that this man was the greatest of all the men of the East.'* He was a rich man and he also had favor in God's sight because he feared God and stayed away from evil. Job had it all, but something struck his life. Listen, it was so bad that his own wife looked at him and thought it was better for him to die, than to live the life he was living. It was terrible! Job lost all that he had, even his own good health, and death would not come for him. He looked around him and there was no single living proof that he was the same person who had all the riches, lands, and livestock as before. But what did Job do in all of this? The Bible says in Job 1:20-22, *'Then Job arose, and rent his mantle, and shaved his head, and fell down upon the ground, and worshipped. And said, Naked came I out from my mother's womb, and naked shall I return thither. the LORD gave, and the LORD hath taken away; Blessed be the name of the LORD."*

*In all this Job did, he did not sin nor charge God with wrong.'* Job stayed true to God! He understood that even if everything was taken from him in the twinkle of an eye, God was able to give it all back even in less time. No, it was not easy for Job! He often wondered why tragedy would befall him in that manner, like in Job 10:1-4, he laments saying, *'"My soul is weary of my life; I will leave my complaint upon myself; I will speak in the bitterness of my soul. I will say to God, Do not condemn me; Shew me wherefore thou contendest with me. Is it good unto thee that thou shouldest oppress, that thou shouldest despise the work of thine hands, and shine upon the counsel of the wicked?'* It was hard for him to comprehend, very hard to accept too. However, Job decided that he would trust in God, and whatever it was that He planned to do through his situation of testing.

### 2. David

The life of David is one that we, as children of God, should study and pick out very important lessons from. King David was not always a king. He started out as a young boy who was seemingly pushed aside to tend to his father's sheep while his brothers went out to do 'more important things.' David stayed in his place, in the season that he was in, and learned all that he needed to learn from the time at hand. David learned how to protect every single one of his father's sheep, and it was this knowledge that gave him the upper hand in being able to kill the great giant, Goliath. God is very intentional; I will say this so many times because His ways are not the ways of man. Also, even when there was a king on the throne of Israel, David was anointed as king. He faced many torments from King Saul who was jealous of little David and even went as far as trying to kill him. These torments gave David sleepless nights; the running and hiding, tired him out and made him cry out to God in prayer many times. David could have killed Saul; he had the chance and the ability to put his trials to an end, but he did not. He left it all in the hands of God. The book of Psalms (which was written by King David), having so many songs of praise to God, is also filled with so many cries for help. Psalm 142:1-7 says, *'I cried unto the LORD with my voice; with my voice unto the LORD did I make my supplication. I poured out my complaint before Him; I shewed before Him my trouble. When my spirit was overwhelmed within me, then thou knewest my path. In the way wherein I walked have they privily laid a snare for me. I looked on my right hand, and beheld, but there was no man that would know me; refuge failed me; no man cared for my soul. I cried unto thee, O LORD: I said, thou art my refuge and my portion in the land of the living. Attend unto my cry, for I am brought very low; deliver me from my persecutors; for they are stronger than I. Bring my soul out of prison, that I may praise thy name; the righteous shall compass me about, for thou shalt deal bountifully with me.'* The pain in this passage of his song is evident, and we can see that as glorious as his life became, he too faced many seasons that were not completely favorable. Eventually, without him raising one finger, God took out his greatest enemy, Saul, in the most mysterious way. Saul fell on his own sword, so that he would not be captured in a battle. The Book of Psalms ended in praise, reading, *'Praise the LORD! Praise God in His sanctuary; Praise Him in the firmament of His power. Praise Him for His mighty acts; Praise Him according to His excellent greatness! Praise Him with the sound of the trumpet; Praise Him with the psaltery and harp! Praise Him with the timbrel and dance; Praise Him with stringed instruments and organs! Praise Him upon the loud cymbals; praise Him upon the high-sounding cymbals. Let everything that has breath praise the LORD. Praise ye the LORD,'* (Psalms 150) so we can see that despite his season of trial, in the end, David rejoiced, and his season of testing had passed.

### 3. Moses.

When God ordains a man to be great, nothing can come in the way. It may seem like you are walking down a lonely path with terror-filled air, but God is right by your side. You may look at yourself, where you are at, and what it is that you have to offer, and nothing seems to be adding up. You look at yourself, then look at others, and you are sure that there are better people to achieve or reach certain heights in life, not you. But that is only the way man thinks. The Bible says in 1 Samuel 16:7 *'But the LORD said to Samuel, Look not on his countenance, or on the height of his stature; because I have refused him: For the LORD seeth not as man seeth; for man looketh on the outward appearance, but the LORD looketh on the heart."'*

In fact, Moses was a stammerer. Exodus 4:10 says, *'And Moses said unto the LORD, O my Lord, I am not eloquent, neither heretofore, nor since thou hast spoken unto thy servant: but I am slow of speech, and of a slow tongue.'* In his heart, he felt like he would be unable to speak to the people of God, and that He was not the right man for the job. Yet, he failed to realize that it was the same God that saved him as a child from the hands of Pharaoh, who was telling him to lead the children of Israel out of Egypt.

In the hands of these same people, Moses was met with various trials and setbacks, from the walk to the murmuring and complaining. He persisted and trusted God, and although he was unable to lead them into the Promised Land, his walk with them in the wilderness was a high point in his life, being the mouthpiece of God to his people. In His obedience, God was glorified.

### 4. Daniel and his friends.

The story of these four strong men, is one that still moves me, it allows me to contemplate and wonder about the greatness of God. Listen, no matter where you are in the curve of life, be it at the lowest point, or worse than that, God can and will show up for you, if you trust Him to. God never forsakes His own! Deuteronomy 31:6 says, *'Be strong and of a good courage, fear not, nor be afraid of them: for the Lord thy God, He it is that doth go with thee; He will not fail thee, nor forsake thee.'* This statement rings true! The Word of God never fails us. Daniel, Shadrach, Meshach, and Abednego were four men who refused to bend their backs in trying to survive their trial. They lived in a city where the king ordered that no one was to worship another God but his god, but they continued serving and praying to the one true God. Their trial came face to face with them, a sentence of death! Yet, these young men refused to bend their backs, or give in to the orders that conflicted with their beliefs. They understood that God would be intentional in shining His light through their time of testing and tribulation. If they did not persist in their difficulties, King Nebuchadnezzar would have never declared that the Almighty God is King. Daniel 3:28-29 says, *'Then Nebuchadnezzar spake, and said, Blessed be the God of Shadrach, Meshach, and Abed-Nego, who hath sent His Angel and delivered His servants that trusted in Him, and have changed the king's word, and yielded their bodies, that they might not serve nor worship any god, except their own God. Therefore I make a decree, that every people, nation, and language, which speak any thing amiss against the God of Shadrach, Meshach, and Abed-Nego, shall be cut in pieces, and their houses shall be made a dunghill: because there is no other God that can deliver after this sort.'*

### 5. Peter

There are sometimes when we feel like we are not worthy to be used by God. This is yet another kind of trial. Perhaps, you feel as though you have no worthy addition to the Kingdom of Heaven, or that you are not the kind of person that deserves mercy. That is the voice of the devil in your head, telling you there is no remedy for where you are, and that you deserve the pain you are experiencing as your final judgment. Again, do not forget that God is not man, and man is not God. When you think God will turn His back on you, He comes running towards you!

Peter is a classic example of such a man. Mark 14:27-31 says, *'And Jesus saith unto them, All ye shall be offended because of me this night: for it is written, I will smite the shepherd, and the sheep shall be scattered. But after that I am risen, I will go before you into*

*Galilee. But Peter said unto him, Although all shall be offended, yet will not I. And Jesus saith unto him, Verily I say unto thee, That this day, even in this night, before the cock crow twice, thou shalt deny me thrice. But he spake the more vehemently, If I should die with thee, I will not deny thee in any wise. Likewise also said they all.'* Peter was sure to his bones that he would not deny Jesus. You can imagine the shame and pain he felt when he finally did! It pushed him to a wall and Mark 14:72 tells us that, he wept when he remembered what Jesus had said.

Peter thought of himself as unworthy and decides that he wants to return to his old job of fishing at the sea. But what happened? John 21:15-25 reads thus:

*'So when they had dined, Jesus saith to Simon Peter, Simon, son of Jonas, lovest thou me more than these? He saith unto him, Yea, Lord; thou knowest that I love thee. He saith unto him, Feed my lambs. He saith to him again the second time, Simon, son of Jonas, lovest thou me? He saith unto him, Yea, Lord; thou knowest that I love thee. He saith unto him, Feed my sheep. He saith unto him the third time, Simon, son of Jonas, lovest thou me? Peter was grieved because he said unto him the third time, Lovest thou me? And he said unto him, Lord, thou knowest all things; thou knowest that I love thee. Jesus saith unto him, Feed my sheep. Verily, verily, I say unto thee, When thou wast young, thou girdest thyself, and walkedst whither thou wouldest: but when thou shalt be old, thou shalt stretch forth thy hands, and another shall gird thee, and carry thee whither thou wouldest not. This spake he, signifying by what death he should glorify God. And when he had spoken this, he saith unto him, Follow me. Then Peter, turning about, seeth the disciple whom Jesus loved following; which also leaned on his breast at supper, and said, Lord, which is he that*

*betrayeth thee? Peter seeing him saith to Jesus, Lord, and what shall this man do? Jesus saith unto him, If I will that he tarry till I come, what is that to thee? follow thou me. Then went this saying abroad among the brethren, that that disciple should not die: yet Jesus said not unto him, He shall not die; but, If I will that he tarry till I come, what is that to thee? This is the disciple which testifieth of these things, and wrote these things: and we know that his testimony is true. And there are also many other things which Jesus did, the which, if they should be written every one, I suppose that even the world itself could not contain the books that should be written. Amen.'*

Peter was restored by Jesus! Listen, brethren, God wants to work in you and through you. The tough times you face now may seem like they will never go away, but I assure you that God has your back. In that crisis, there will be a birthing. You must never let a crisis go to waste. Be patient enough and put your ears on God's heart, so you can hear all He has to say about that season of your life. Remember, seasons will come, and seasons will go. Season in and season out. Each specific period, will prepare you for the next, so what are you learning right now?

## The Life of Paul.

*'Knowing that a man is not justified by the works of the law but by faith in Jesus Christ, even we have believed in Christ Jesus, that we might be justified by faith in Christ and not by the works of the law; for by the works of the law no flesh shall be justified,'* Galatians 2:16.

The life we live, as Christians, is not a 'start to finish' kind of life. It does not happen that you start out as a little kitten and because of your faith in God, you automatically become a lion, no. The Christian life is majorly a life of conversion, change, faith, and acceptance. As Christians, this is one thing we are constantly in pursuit of, the very foundation of the religion, our conviction, of our beliefs. This is because if we believe in God, in the gift of His son, and in the potency of the sacrifice made on the cross, then our lives can be changed radically. Conversion is what happens when a person changes their belief and decides to follow God. It is a miracle that happens when God comes into the life of a person and changes everything, turning it all around so that the person never remains the same. Conversion is saying, 'I may have been this in the past, but I know that by the cleansing power of the blood of Jesus, I am now this.'

The life of Paul is something that I would encourage every Christian to study and understand fully in their walk with Christ. In fact, each time I hear the word 'tribulation,' my mind first goes to the Apostle Paul and everything that he suffered and endured for the sake of the Kingdom of God. In the Book of 2nd Corinthians, Paul delves into the many sufferings that he endured in the ministry of the gospel of Christ. 2 Corinthians 11:22-29 says, *'Are they Hebrews? so am I. Are they Israelites? so am I. Are they the seed of Abraham? so am I. Are they ministers of Christ? (I speak as a fool) I am more; in labours more abundant, in stripes above measure, in prisons more frequent, in deaths oft. Of the Jews five times received I forty stripes save one. Thrice was I beaten with rods, once was I stoned, thrice I suffered shipwreck, a night and a day I have been in the deep; In journeyings often, in perils of waters, in perils of robbers, in perils by mine own countrymen, in perils by the heathen, in perils in the city, in perils in the wilderness, in perils in the sea, in perils among false brethren; In weariness and painfulness, in watchings often, in hunger and thirst, in fastings often, in cold and nakedness. Beside those things that are without, that which cometh upon me daily, the care of all the churches. Who is weak, and I am not weak? who is offended, and I burn not?'*

His sufferings were many! Paul was a man that was very knowledgeable about the laws of the city. He grew up in a family that enforced the law, an entire family of Pharisees, so you can imagine how spent his life must have been. He grew up to be the head persecutor of Christians, approving their deaths (like the stoning of Steven, the martyr). He was on his way to Damascus to arrest Christians when he was 'seized' by Christ Jesus. That was the beginning of his conversion, the beginning of a change in his life.

Now, there are so many things that can go wrong if you can imagine. Let us assume a person who has been arresting Christians walks up to you one day and says he would like to know more about your religion. It sounds like part of a bigger plan, right? Exactly! First, Paul's conversion was not easily accepted by other Christians because they could not understand how the one who once killed them was now on their side. Next, Paul's family and his co-prosecutors were out for him, leaving him stuck in such a tight place and a 'fertile ground' for intense tribulations. For the former, God let them know in Acts 9:15-16 that he was on their side, saying, *'But the Lord said to him, "But the Lord said unto him, Go thy way: for he is a chosen vessel unto me, to bear my name before the Gentiles, and kings, and the children of Israel: For I will shew him how great things he must suffer for my name's sake.'* Paul did suffer greatly, but he knew how important that suffering was in shaping him, and in building the Church of Christ. He went for ministries, building churches, and preaching the gospel. He traveled to so many places for the sake of the gospel, such as Galatia, Syria, Macedonia, Achaia, Corinth, Jerusalem, and Antioch, suffering great trials in each of these places. He worked very hard and gave all the glory of his works to God, even while suffering and enduring persecution himself, some of the laws being those that he enforced before his conversion. He was imprisoned in Caesarea, Rome, and also in Philippi. The beatings were so much that he could not even write on all of them. He said in 2 Corinthians 1:8-9, *'For we would not, brethren, have you ignorant of our trouble which came to us in Asia, that we were pressed out of measure, above strength, insomuch that we despaired even of life: But we had the sentence of death in ourselves, that we should not trust in ourselves, but in God which raiseth the dead.'*

If we go into the details of these punishments, we will see how some of them could have been avoided very easily. That is, some of the punishments were laws, Jewish laws. If he wished, he could have not abided, but that would have meant his being cut off from the rest of the Jews. If this had happened, Paul would have been unable to preach the gospel of Christ to the Jews. He suffered for the sake of the Kingdom because he knew he was laying up his treasures in Heaven, where the season of joy would never come to an end. We could go on and on to explain the agony, trials, and tribulations that Paul endured. A major part of the New Testament talks about his life and his ministry. He endured for righteousness' sake, trusting God to deliver him in a way he could never deliver himself. What have you learned from the life of Paul and his writings? Do you get comfort when you revisit his trials and then compare them with whatever it is you may be experiencing? Do you get any hope knowing that a man who could be beaten, persecuted, and imprisoned, could matter so much to the Kingdom of God? He was empowered by God, and so can you. Be empowered today, knowing that your season serves a purpose.

You must never doubt the extent of God's love for you. You are His treasure, His creation. It brings Him no delight seeing you in pain, confusion, and sorrow, but when those come, do not be quick to sulk in it. Instead, find out the importance and sole purpose of that season, and live it to the fullest.

Before I close this chapter, I want to share my testimony with you. I pray it will help you in your times of need. When I reflect back on my life, it was only God who brought me through. There was so much pain and abuse from a young age that followed me into my adult life. The passing of my mother when I was only 17 years old and my first marriage being abusive, these trials have given me victory. In spite of persecution, health prognosis, finances, ridicule, and lies, God has lifted my head and plucked me out of the fire. I am a brand plucked from the fire, going through the pain and agony that many women face daily.

I lost my younger sister when she was in her early 30s to breast cancer. I have a son in prison, although he is now ministering as a pastor. Though confined, I am glad that he is helping to save souls. In spite of the heartache of his absence, I still believe, and I am trusting God for his physical freedom.

So, you see, I know all about suffering. I know all about struggling and working to overcome issues, because there have been so many storms in my own life. I realize that when you are going through struggles, it can be very overwhelming, and things can get so cloudy that you don't see a way out. I didn't always see a way out, because I was blinded by my pain and frustration, as a mother and a pastor. My own children had gone astray, disobeying God and bringing shame to Christ's name.

Do not think doing God's work is going to be easy, as you stand up for righteousness and truth. Living a life pursuing God, and speaking His truth will make you a target for the enemy (1 Peter 4:12-13, 1 Corinthians 10:13). However, I can testify today that while in life, we may go through some storms, I assure you that after the calm of the storm, the sun will shine. Troubles don't last always, only for a season. So whatever season you are in, be mindful to **REJOICE** and **BE HAPPY!**

God gave me a word: In Deuteronomy 31:6, it says to be strong and of good courage, fear not. He said, "I am with you. I will not forsake you." Our deliverance is in the Word. You are going to have seasons in your life that seem impossible or overwhelming. There will be seasons of joy and seasons of trouble, but whatever stage God has you in; you have to choose to make the best of it. You have to be determined to search the scriptures, build up your own faith and encourage yourself. Remember, good fruit and harvest can still manifest out of your hardships.

Dr. Brenda Jefferson

## CHAPTER TWO

## JESUS, OUR HOPE IN AGES PAST

*'Even the youths shall faint and be weary, and the young men shall utterly fall: But they that wait upon the* LORD *shall renew their strength; they shall mount up with wings as eagles; they shall run, and not be weary; and they shall walk, and not faint,'* Isaiah 40:30-31.

There is a story that I've heard so many times in the past, especially while growing up. For some time, it was just for the enjoyment of it that I listened to and told the story to other people, but now, I am older and wiser, and I can say that this story is important to grasp what trust in God really looks like.

The story starts in a small village, where no mother was educated and every father was a farmer or a fisherman, there had been no rain for a very long time. The crops were dying, the water wells were drying up slowly, and the heat of the day chased the fish to the bottom of the river. The leaders had gathered together respectively but none of their plans seemed to work out. During one of their meetings when all hope had been lost, a young man suggested that they call the attention of a rainmaker. After much discussion, they did so. The rainmaker was brought down to the village within the hour, and he called the attention of all the people living in the village, young and old.

"By this same time in the morrow, you shall all gather here and wait for the rains. And it shall come!" the rainmaker said.

There was great joy in the village, and everyone waited in anticipation. Then the next day came. Sara was a little kid and the only child of her both parents. She joined her father and mother to prepare for the trip to the square where the people were told to gather.

"What is that for?" Sara's mother asked as they started to leave their home.

Sara looked down at the umbrella she was holding in her hands and stared back at her mother with faith-filled eyes.

"The rains will come today," Sara said.

---

Similarly, there are instances in scripture where God instructed the wind, storms ceased at His commands, and even Elijah stopped the rain (1 Kings 17-18; Mark 4:39). Life is already as hard as it can get, child-like faith can make all the difference. We have some periods of uncertainty and pain that come our way, and many times we just want to throw in the towel and say, *'you know what, I am done with this,'* but what good will that be? Every single one of us needs hope, both in old age and at every other point in our lives. The world itself is filled with so much uncertainty, diseases, illnesses, poverty, wars, poverty, oppression, and even death. All of this starts right from the conception of life, until the very end. So, what good will it bring a man to put hope in Earthly things? From pregnancy, a mother will have a series of tests done to make sure her little one is fine. She would eat as healthy as she can, so that the fetus can get all the nutrition it needs and some more. From birth, the parents carefully dedicate their time to ensuring the safety and comfort of the baby, placing a monitor in the crib where the child sleeps, watching, and caring all day and night. All of these and even extra, do not take away from the fact that tragedy could still happen to that child, in the midst of all the safety, prevention, and prayers. Every single one of us needs a hope that we can hold on to, in the times when our practical strategies fail us (because they are bound to).

Hope is a feeling of expectation and desire for a particular thing to happen. It is a feeling of trust. As Christians, our lives and all that involve us are expected to revolve around one thing, and that is *hope*. To have hope in God is to trust Him to give us the future that we have been promised in His Word. Now, this may sound easy for the books and for the records, but you know it does not get to be that straightforward when we are faced with situations and realities that seem to go south. Many times, certain things come our way that makes us doubt the authenticity and potency of the promises of God. Let us take a look at the Children of Israel again. From their story filled with grievances and grumbles, we can see that they lacked hope in God, and in turn, did not trust that God will lead them to the land that He had promised them. A lack of hope can arise from a place of 'satisfaction,' but also from a lack of knowledge and unbelief.

Let us look at the case of someone who has been a junior staff in the office for so long, earning about 15 dollars per hour with no leave and no bonuses. Then somehow, he hears clearly from God that he will be promoted and earn 60 dollars per hour for the rest of the year. He is very excited and begins to prepare himself for this promotion. Then, he gets queried at work, and it was almost unavoidable. He returns to his workspace and laughs at himself saying "look at you thinking you could be a senior soon!" He loses hope and continues to work in his current role as junior staff, having no desire to 'stress' for something, since he could not have it anyway. He has become very comfortable with his role as a junior staff. He has probably been able to survive on his salary, just enough to keep himself fed, housed, and out of debt, and so he sees no need for the bother.

He is equally quite uninformed of the place that he could be, and the blessings that are involved with the higher place or position (more work, more pay, and some more work), so he does not bother to go after it. In his complacency, he could have missed a viable opportunity. How many times do we stay in our present situation for fear of the unknown?

This was the story of the Egyptians. They continually complained about all of the obstacles they met along the way, be it before they crossed the red sea, or in the wilderness. They had suffered terribly as slaves in Egypt but because they had become comfortable and satisfied with their pain and suffering, they saw it as a better option than to go after their own land promised to them by God. If they were not ignorant of the gift in the Promised Land waiting for them, perhaps they would have endured. Nevertheless, hope does not require that we see first, it requires that we TRUST! *"For we walk by faith, not by sight,"* (2 Corinthians 5:7). Yes, the world is evil! We are in trying times when it is hard to find solace in any of the events around us. The economies of nations are crumbling, leaders are failing, and countries are fighting, but there has not been a time when everything was completely peaceful. As far back as the time of Jesus, there was a man called Simeon who had been waiting for hope. He was waiting for something firm to hold on to, for the sake of Israel and the Holy Spirit revealed to him that he would not die, until he receives this hope he so wanted. Luke 2:25-35 reads:

*'And, behold, there was a man in Jerusalem, whose name was Simeon; and the same man was just and devout, waiting for the consolation of Israel: and the Holy Ghost was upon him. And it was revealed unto him by the Holy Ghost, that he should not see death, before he had seen the Lord's Christ. And he came by the Spirit into the temple: and when the parents brought in the child Jesus, to do for him after the custom of the law, Then took he him up in his arms, and blessed God, and said, Lord, now lettest thou thy servant depart in peace, according to thy word: For mine eyes have seen thy salvation, Which thou hast prepared before the face of all people; A light to lighten the Gentiles, and the glory of thy people Israel. And Joseph and his mother marvelled at those things which were spoken of him. And Simeon blessed them, and said unto Mary his mother, Behold, this child is set for the fall and rising again of many in Israel; and for a sign which shall be spoken against; (Yea, a sword shall pierce through thy own soul also,) that the thoughts of many hearts may be revealed.'*

## Seasons

We have our hope! From what Simeon did and said, we have one thing known for sure; As long as we place our hope in Jesus Christ and in the promises of God, we will not be forsaken, and we will be rewarded. We have been told that for the debt of our own sins, a price has been paid by the sacrifice of the only Son of God, Jesus Christ, on the Cross of Cavalry. Did you know that to hope means to have faith in the authenticity and power of this sacrifice? Let us take it back a little bit. The Bible says in John 6:26-40:

*'Jesus answered them and said, Verily, verily, I say unto you, Ye seek me, not because ye saw the miracles, but because ye did eat of the loaves, and were filled. Labour not for the meat which perisheth, but for that meat which endureth unto everlasting life, which the Son of man shall give unto you: for him hath God the Father sealed. Then said they unto him, What shall we do, that we might work the works of God? Jesus answered and said unto them, This is the work of God, that ye believe on him whom he hath sent. They said therefore unto him, What sign shewest thou then, that we may see, and believe thee? what dost thou work? Our fathers did eat manna in the desert; as it is written, He gave them bread from heaven to eat. Then Jesus said unto them, Verily, verily, I say unto you, Moses gave you not that bread from heaven; but my Father giveth you the true bread from heaven. For the bread of God is he which cometh down from heaven, and giveth life unto the world. Then said they unto him, Lord, evermore give us this bread. And Jesus said unto them, I am the bread of life: he that cometh to me shall never hunger; and he that believeth on me shall never thirst. But I said unto you, That ye also have seen me, and believe not. All that the Father giveth me shall come to me; and him that cometh to me I will in no wise cast out. For I came down from heaven, not to do mine own will, but the will of him that sent*

*me. And this is the Father's will which hath sent me, that of all which he hath given me I should lose nothing, but should raise it up again at the last day. And this is the will of him that sent me, that every one which seeth the Son, and believeth on him, may have everlasting life: and I will raise him up at the last day.'*

Jesus let the people know that everyone who sees Him and believes that He is the Messiah, will have everlasting life. They will have their hope! It is written in so many other parts of the Bible, that Jesus Christ is the only way to the Father. How do we establish this gift? By believing! It is not enough to say 'I believe in the power of the blood of Jesus that was shed for my sins,' you must have a clear conviction in your spirit. A way that we can truly express our hope in Christ, is to live in the manner that we have been asked to, just like our Father in Heaven. 1 John 3:10 says, *'In this the children of God are manifest, and the children of the devil: whosoever doeth not righteousness is not of God, neither he that loveth not his brother.'* You cannot claim to believe in the life of Jesus Christ, and contrarily your actions do not align with His Word. That is a distinct lack of faith in the power of God.

To have hope in Jesus Christ means to be righteous in your way of life, and expectant of the power of God and the Holy Spirit. Simeon was said to be a man who was 'just and devout.' This means that Simeon acted right to his fellow man and his ways showed that he was after the heart of God, looking to please God in all his ways. He trusted God to send down hope, and he obeyed the commandments of God, even when no one was watching.

To be devout means to have or show deep religious feelings or commitment, and to be totally committed to a cause or belief. Simeon was completely committed to his spiritual life and religion. You know that this is not bestowed on someone, right? No one is blessed with the gift of being devout; they build it! Simeon cultivated his life to breathe and show righteousness. Reading the passage over and over again, we can see how much Simeon humbled himself and placed God far above in reverence. There were no prophets in Israel at the time, Simeon lived, and the leaders were entirely political with no traces of spirituality. So, Simeon had plausible reason to give up on his hope that seemed so far away, but he chose to trust in God.

If we truly have our hope in Jesus Christ our Lord, we must be sure to live righteous lives. We have hope because we believe in His power and we plant our feet in His footprints, in hopes to be saved on the last day. There is a condition; to live just as we have been commanded. If we do not meet up with this condition, then our hope is 'hopeless.'

To have our hope in Christ is also to have faith in His power. The story above, speaks of a little girl who could have simply gone to the gathering like everyone else just to 'see' what would happen, but with her, there were no buts! She knew it would happen. She believed that the season of dryness would be over, and she prepared for it by gathering her umbrella. To have hope in Christ, we must live with a conviction in our spirits that He will come through for us in at the time appropriate. When we read the short passage above, we see that Simeon was very expectant. Verse 25 says that he was 'waiting for the consolation of Israel.' Now, that is hope! There had been no single prophet in Israel for up to 400 years. So basically, Simeon had waited all of his life for Jesus Christ to be born, for hope to shine down on Israel. It would have been so easy for him to say 'oh, this did not happen 10 years ago, and it did not happen even two hundred years ago. I should give up and move on.' But no, he persisted with his expectation, and he eventually received it.

So, do you live with expectations in your heart? Do you trust that when you pray, God will answer your prayers? Do you have faith that all the promises made by God in His Word will be yours in good time? The Bible says in Hebrew 11:6, *'But without faith, it is impossible to please Him, for he that cometh to God must believe that He is, and that He is a rewarder of them that diligently seek Him.'* How do you please God if you do not believe in His power? This is the very core of our religion! Look around at your circumstances and then internally reflect as well; do you trust in God and His power, or do you judge based on the look of things, events, and circumstances? Will Jesus be able to find faith in you by the time He returns? (Luke 18:8).

To have hope in God, is to accept the timing and power of the Holy Spirit. Simeon was assisted and guided by the Holy Spirit. The Holy Spirit revealed many things to him, and that is how it has always been in the past. When Jesus was leaving, He said, *'And I will pray the Father, and He shall give you another Comforter, that He may abide with you for ever,'* (John 14:16) and *'But the Comforter, which is the Holy Ghost, whom the Father will send in my name, he shall teach you all things, and bring all things to your remembrance, whatsoever I have said unto you,'* (John 14:26).

In Holiness, we must realize that Jesus Christ has given us the gift of the Holy Spirit, and not utilizing this gift is a lack of hope in God. We simply do not trust in the potency of this Helper that He has given to us, as we should. Ask yourself a question; if today, God chose to take away His Holy Spirit from you, would there be any difference? Would you feel a void in your life, or will you carry on as though nothing has happened or changed? We need to depend on the Holy Spirit and acknowledge him in all that we do. You must depend on his guidance and instructions for our day-to-day living. The Holy Spirit is your guide and your help; you should trust in him to help you live a life that is pleasing to God. You should seek his face when you need help with resisting temptations, when you need insights for living, when you are face-to-face with challenging times and seasons of your life, or when you are in a tight corner and forced to make difficult decisions.

Apostle Paul made it clear that it is by the power of the Holy Spirit that we can live in hope. He said in Romans 15:13, *'Now the God of hope fill you with all joy and peace in believing, that ye may abound in hope, through the power of the Holy Ghost.'* Learn to live in the fullness of the Spirit of God, and the Lord will fill your heart with true joy, love, peace, and faith. This is exactly what we all need when the devil pokes up his head and tries to fill our hearts with doubt, anxiety, depression, and despair during our tough seasons of trials and tribulations. Be sensitive towards the Holy Spirit and if you do not have him, ask the Lord daily that He blesses you with this gift that surpasses what we can ever think of. While asking, make your heart and life a place where the Holy Spirit can dwell. Remember, he is Holy, so you must be Holy to have him.

To hope in Christ, aside from the obvious peace that it brings in the middle of a storm has great benefits. There is a reward for those who trust in God because it is God we are speaking of, the maker of the Heavens and the Earth, not a man! A man who has his hope in Christ Jesus, will be rewarded with a great and unmatchable understanding of the things pertaining to God and His Kingdom, and this will always come in handy in navigating through life. A person with an understanding of the things of God will know the right time to move and act. They will have peace of mind in the middle of the storm, just like Jesus Christ was, and they will not be swayed left and right by difficulties. When we put our hope in Christ, we are also rewarded with a divine understanding of spiritual affairs. It takes a man who understands the law of order and the workings of the Father to expect something he has not seen, in so many ages. To a mere man, he is stupid and 'unrealistic' but to God, he is wise and he will be rewarded.

Another reward to your faith is the fulfillment of your desires (as long as they are in line with the will of God for you). As you trust in God, you do not just make Him 'feel' powerful, but you allow Him to *be* powerful in your life. A reward of hope is an answer to your prayers and the manifestation of the good things you desire. The Bible says in Psalm 34:10 *"The young lions do lack, and suffer*

*hunger: but they that seek the Lord shall not want any good thing."*
Hope combined with faith in God, increases our endurance level to produce the desired outcome God expects of us. Anything less than this leads to defeat and mediocrity and God has not called any of His children to live a mediocre life. Simeon was granted what he desired because he hoped for it. He said clearly that he was ready to die because his long-time desire had now been fulfilled. A couple of verses in the Bible confirm this.

- Delight yourself also in the LORD, and He shall give you the desires of your heart - *Psalm 37:4*
- The young lions do lack and suffer hunger, but those who seek the LORD shall not lack any good thing - *Psalm 34:10*
- For the LORD God *is* a sun and shield; the LORD will give grace and glory; no good *thing* will He withhold from those who walk uprightly - *Psalm 84:11*

God is a loving father and a merciful King. He will never go back on His Word, nor will He leave you by yourself. All you need to do is to place your hope in Him, have faith in His Word and His promises, and He will bless you.

One thing that is sure for those who have their hope in God, is a readiness for death. As you may already know, the end of 'life' is not just death, but eternal life for those who believe in and follow the ways of God. In salvation, we don't really die but instead pass from death unto life (John 5:24). Simeon announced that he was ready to die. This is because he lived a righteous life and had his hope in God.

The truth is, no one is ever really 'ready to die' if they have not seen Jesus. That is, if they have not turned their face to Him and looked up to Him for mercy and cleansing. We are born sinners, and this will only change when we accept Christ as our Lord and savior. Until then, a person is not ready for death. There is nothing that this life has to offer any one of us. Our true hope is in the eternal life that comes right after, which we can only access through Jesus Christ, the only Son of God.

## Following the footsteps of Jesus and focusing on the Kingdom of God

If you have a child, or you have closely watched a child grow from a young age, you see one thing for sure; they are a product of their environment. The things that they watch, see, and listen to are very big determinants of what they eventually become. Some use the term humans 'sponges,' soaking in the things in our environment. As children of God the situation is the same, but to truly follow in the footsteps of Jesus, we need to be selective sponges.

*1 Peter 2:21-25 says, 'For even hereunto were ye called: because Christ also suffered for us, leaving us an example, that ye should follow his steps: who did no sin, neither was guile found in his mouth: who, when he was reviled, reviled not again; when he suffered, he threatened not; but committed himself to him that judgeth righteously: who his own self bare our sins in his own body on the tree, that we, being dead to sins, should live unto righteousness: by whose stripes ye were healed. For ye were as sheep going astray; but are now returned unto the Shepherd and Bishop of your souls.'*

Peter advises that we live our lives with one question on our minds; **'What would Jesus do?'** Jesus, the Son of God, was sent down to Earth from Heaven to do the work of the Father. No, He did not have it easy, in fact, the burden was great enough for him to ask that it is taken away from him. Matthew 26:39 reads, *'And he went a little farther, and fell on his face, and prayed, saying, O my Father, if it be possible, let this cup pass from me: nevertheless not as I will, but as thou wilt.'* It was a life filled with temptations, trials, and tribulations, yet Jesus Christ endured and did the will of God. This is what God demands from you and me. We are asked to look to Jesus and follow His steps because if He is the only way to the Father, then we would be on track to living life just as He did while on Earth. There are so many different traits of Christ that we should emulate; He was patient, loving, respectful and polite, peaceful, caring, and above all, He had the will of the Father at the core of His heart. When we are faced with hard situations, we should always look to Jesus as the one to emulate. While Jesus was having such a hard time, being beaten, spat on, crucified, lied against, and judged, what did He do? He chose to forgive His persecutors and even pray for them.

These are the ways that we should follow, rather than allow for anger, hatred, and bitterness to eat up our hearts when we come face to face with difficult seasons of our lives. We can find out about the life of Jesus Christ on Earth, in the Bible, and this is why we must always refer to the scriptures as our manual for living.

Follow the instructions daily, listen to the voice of the Holy Spirit, and learn the ways of Jesus Christ. The more frequently you do this, the more aligned you become with the will of God. Is it not a great blessing that you do not have to figure life out on your own? Yes, it is!

We must be very intentional about what we allow into our hearts. The Bible tells us to guard our hearts with diligence because out of it, the issues of life will flow. Also, the ideas we allow to grow in our hearts determine the pattern of our thoughts. When faced with a difficult situation, rather than speak negative words about the situation, speak life. The Bible teaches about the power of the tongue, so if the tongue can bring evil and good, then we must use it for good. We need to train our minds to see the good in every situation. It is optimism, and optimism is simply hoping for the best. Speak life to yourself, speak life to the situation that you find yourself in, speak life into the people around you, and watch everything come alive, just as God wants for you and for me.

Trusting God is not a destination, but a journey in which we continue to press ahead daily. The hope of God endures forever, and He is our surest shield. The promises of God do not always mean easy for each of us. There are instances in this moment, where a fellow brother at work, school, or church may be feeling very hopeless and confused about the state of his life. He may have tried over and over again to make a particular thing work in his favor, but all to no gain. You are there for a reason, and that is to pull him up and help to restore his hope and strength in the reviving and resurrection power of God. Your words and your actions are powerful enough to restore hope. Encourage somebody else today.

Even Jesus Christ was an encouragement to the church in John 16:33 which says, *'These things I have spoken unto you, that in me ye might have peace. In the world ye shall have tribulation: but be of good cheer; I have overcome the world.'* God commands us in His Word to be a source of encouragement to one another, not because He simply wants to enforce a decree, but because encouragement gives life, clear hope, and a reason to continue in the journey of service to God and man. The world is not run by the devil especially as we have been given the power to overcome the enemy, yet his devices are such that try to leave us broken and sinful, killing our dreams, and weakening our hearts. For this reason, we must pull ourselves up. When there is no encouragement and there is no hope in the love of God, people feel unloved and forsaken. God encourages us to be a source of hope to one another until His Son returns. Every single thing we do as children of God, should prepare us for eternal life in the Kingdom of God. The devil will do all that he can to keep us far from this goal, but we must stay true to it, drawing strength from God and His Word.

**The Promises of God.**

*'If a son shall ask bread of any of you that is a father, will he give him a stone? or if he ask a fish, will he for a fish give him a serpent? Or if he shall ask an egg, will he offer him a scorpion? If ye then, being evil, know how to give good gifts unto your children: how much more shall your Heavenly Father give the Holy Spirit to them that ask him?'* Luke 11:11-13.

When I think of my life as a child of God, I count myself blessed and highly favored. From the very beginning of creation, God has had me in mind. Everything that a God, so great and mighty does is with intention to give me the best in life. Nothing is more comforting to know, than this! That every day, from when I wake up to when I lay my head to rest, God is working in me and for me, to give me a desired future. What a privilege this is! As children of God, what gives us the confidence to live a happy life in this cold, dark, and gruesome world? No, we do not trust in our own power, in our riches, or in our wisdom. We trust in the Almighty God. He is a good Father who has promised us a good life on Earth and beyond. In His omnipotence, He has an inability to fail. God can never fail, not once has it happened in the past, nor will it ever in the future.

Many will hear these words, but not have confidence in them. There is no way we can have this confidence in God and in His power, if we do not have faith in Him. How do we grow our faith in God? Romans 10:17 says, *'So then faith comes by hearing, and hearing by the Word of God.'* All of the promises from God to each of us are written in the Word of God. He makes it plain. The devil will try to tell you that those promises are not for you, perhaps because of one sin or the other that you may have found yourself in, or for any reasons at all, but I assure you that as long as you are a child of God, and you retrace your steps back to the throne of Grace. Yes, the promises of God are for you.

The Bible says in Joshua 21:43-45, *'And the LORD gave unto Israel all the land which he sware to give unto their fathers; and they possessed it, and dwelt therein. And the LORD gave them rest round about, according to all that he sware unto their fathers: and there stood not a man of all their enemies before them; the LORD delivered all their enemies into their hand.* **There failed not ought of any good thing which the LORD had spoken unto the House of Israel; all came to pass.**' Not even one of God's promises was unfulfilled. You may go ahead to say 'oh, that was for the children of Israel, not me or us today.' Well, I ask you to think on this today: *Are you in or of Israel?* Paul said in Romans 9:6-8, *'Not as though the Word of God hath taken none effect. For they are not all Israel, which are of Israel: Neither, because they are the seed of Abraham, are they all children: but, In Isaac shall thy seed be called. That is, they which are the children of the flesh, these are not the children of God: but the children of the promise are counted for the seed.'* What does this say? Simple. Being born a Jew does not mean an automatic entry into the Kingdom of God. It is those who follow God that are His children, His people. The promises of God are granted in the life of those who intentionally commit their lives to trust Him and do just as He says they should do. The promises of God are real and true, and nothing will make Him go back on His words. There are so many promises we can always tap into.

**- God has promised that He will give you strength.**

Ephesians 3:14-16 says, 'For this cause I bow my knees unto the Father of our Lord Jesus Christ, of whom the whole family in Heaven and Earth is named, that He would grant you, according to the riches of His glory, to be strengthened with might by His Spirit in the inner man.' You do not have to go through your struggles all by yourself. You do not have to bear the pain alone. Yes, they will come, but God says that He will give you the strength that you need to overcome.

**- God has promised to give you true rest.**
Matthew 11:28-30 says, 'Come to Me, all you who labor and are heavy laden, and I will give you rest. Take My yoke upon you and learn from Me, for I am gentle and lowly in heart, and you will find rest for your souls. For My yoke is easy and My burden is light.' When the burden gets too overbearing for you to handle, He says His arms are open unto you so that you can find rest in him.

**- God has promised to provide answers to all your prayers.**

The Bible says in Mark 11:22-24 'And Jesus answering saith unto them, Have faith in God. For verily I say unto you, That whosoever shall say unto this mountain, Be thou removed, and be thou cast into the sea; and shall not doubt in his heart, but shall believe that those things which he saith shall come to pass; he shall have whatsoever he saith. Therefore I say unto you, What things soever ye desire, when ye pray, believe that ye receive them, and ye shall have them.' You must always remember that in God, you have a Father who is always ready to hear from you. Anytime you call on Him, He listens and will be ready to answer, as long as you believe, and you ask in line with His will.

**- God has promised that He will take care of all your needs.**
Philippians 4:19 says, 'And my God shall supply all your need according to His riches in glory by Christ Jesus.' According to His riches in glory is such a powerful phrase, why? For the reason that

God owns it all and can give you anything that your heart desires and greater. He can give you more than you could ever ask or think, at the right time and in the right season.

**- God has promised that everything that happens around you will work for your good.**
This is one of my favorite verses to read; Romans 8:28. It says, 'And we know that all things work together for good to those who love God, to those who are the called according to His purpose.' It gives a calmness when we feel frustrated, and allows us to know that even if we do not see an end or use of the current season we are in, God has a bigger plan.

**-God has promised that He will always be with you.**
Joshua 1:5 says, 'There shall not any man be able to stand before thee all the days of thy life: as I was with Moses, so I will be with thee: I will not fail thee, nor forsake thee.' In the middle of the storm or in the heat of the desert, God says that He will be with you always. He would never leave your side. This should give you the confidence to live life, knowing that you have the presence of God which is always filled with joy and peace.

**- God has said that He will give you freedom from the hold of sin.**
Our God is indeed a merciful God. As much as He rings it in our ears to avoid the devil and any signs of darkness, He is also giving us the power to do it at the same time. He is willing to cleanse our hearts of the evil we were born with and draw us closer to Him so we can see the light. 1 John 1:9 says, 'If we confess our sins, He is faithful and just to forgive us *our* sins and to cleanse us from all

unrighteousness.' And John 8:36 says, 'If we confess our sins, He is faithful and just to forgive us *our* sins and to cleanse us from all unrighteousness.'

**- God has promised to protect you from the evil around your dwelling.**
Psalm 91:1-8 tells us of the kind of stronghold our city will have when God dwells in it. It says, 'He who dwells in the secret place of the Most High shall abide under the shadow of the Almighty. I will say of the LORD, "He is my refuge and my fortress; my God, in Him I will trust." Surely, He shall deliver you from the snare of the fowler and from the perilous pestilence. He shall cover you with His feathers, and under His wings, you shall take refuge; His truth shall be your shield and buckler. You shall not be afraid of the terror by night, nor of the arrow that flies by day, nor of the pestilence that walks in darkness, nor of the destruction that lays waste at noonday. A thousand may fall at your side, and ten thousand at your right hand; but it shall not come near you. Only with your eyes shall you look and see the reward of the wicked.' Praise God!

**- God has promised that there is nothing that can stop Him from loving you.**
Romans 8:38-39 says this clearly, 'For I am persuaded that neither death nor life, nor angels nor principalities nor powers, nor things present nor things to come, nor height nor depth, nor any other created thing, shall be able to separate us from the love of God which is in Christ Jesus our Lord.' So, not even your sins will stop God from loving you. Not the sins of your parents, not your

ignorance, not your lifestyle, nothing at all. You are loved unconditionally, and I expect that this love should make you want to please the Lord.

### - God has promised to grant you everlasting life in Him.

No, not in this cold, dark, and gruesome world, but in His peaceful and loving abode. The Bible says in John 3:16, 'For God so loved the world that He gave His only begotten Son, that whoever believes in Him should not perish but have everlasting life.' There is no gift greater, than life itself.

The promises of God are so much more than this in the entire Bible, and even in our personal spaces where we pray to and hear from God, we get personalized promises for certain situations in our lives. Hold on to these promises! You can write them out, look at them daily, declare them, pray with them, and live in the reality of each of them. When you do this, everything begins to become a reality as God takes the upper hand in your life. Just as 2 Corinthians 1:20 says; 'For all the promises of God in Him are Yes, and in Him Amen, to the glory of God through us' we will see and experience the coming of the promises of God in our lives. Amen.

## Thanksgiving and hope in down times.

*'Rejoice always, pray without ceasing, in everything give thanks; for this is the will of God in Christ Jesus for you,'* 1 Thessalonians 5:16-18.

It does not sound real, right? That a man who has just lost his job is expected to say to God, 'Thank you that I just lost my job', or that a couple having a terrible time in their marriage should remain smiling and giving God thanks, or a father whose child is fighting for his life at the hospital must stay thankful somehow. For many, it just seems so out of this world, but do you know that it is possible? Thanksgiving is more than just an event celebrated in some parts of the world every year. It is more than that; it is the state of the heart of an individual. A person who is thankful does not have to be given a gift before they say thank you. Instead, they are quick to look around themselves and find something to be grateful for, because there will **always** be something to be grateful for during hardship, like life, at the very least.

There is something that a person with a thankful heart possesses that is rare. They can look at their life and see the many things that need to be sorted, to be done, or to be fixed, but a thankful heart understands seasons and says 'even if this may not look so good right now, I know that it will get better. I know that I am loved, and I am blessed, so thank you God for that.'

Thanksgiving is celebrated yearly, but there are many people who believe that there is not much to be thankful for around them. Nevertheless, in your worst seasons in life, that is in fact, the perfect time to cultivate and build a lifestyle of thankfulness and gratitude to God for the blessings He gives. For the sake of your growth, peace, and even sanity, you must learn to build a heart of thanksgiving. Yes, there are many things to feel down about, but can you take a minute to count the blessings of God in your life?

We must learn to be grateful that despite all that happens, we still have a God up there who listens and answers when we call. We have a God that blesses us when we least expect it, and shows up for us when we feel like we have hit a dead end. Do you know that sometimes, God allows for bad to come so that you can see Him work after you pray? The Bible says in Jeremiah 29:7 *'And seek the peace of the city where I have caused you to be carried away captive, and pray to the LORD for it; for in its peace, you will have peace.'* So, when you hit the bottom of the ladder, cry out to God for help, and when He does show up, pour out your heart in thanksgiving.

One thing I say to myself when I sense some kind of lack is 'I operate in the currency of the kingdom of Heaven' because I know that there is no such thing as lack up there. Revelation 21:4 says, *'And God will wipe away every tear from their eyes; there shall be no more death, nor sorrow, nor crying. There shall be no more pain, for the former things have passed away.'* There is freedom for the children of God, so much to be thankful for!

Remember, nothing is too hard for God to handle. Be careful for nothing, but in everything by prayer and supplication with thanksgiving let your request be known unto God. And the peace of God, which passeth all understanding shall keep your hearts and minds through Christ Jesus (Phil 4:6-7). You have to believe that God will make a way, even when you can't see the way at the time. Be like David, he was gently distressed for the people spake of stoning him, because the soul of all the people was grieved, every man for his sons and for his daughters, but David encouraged himself in the Lord his God (1 Sam 30:6). Keep speaking the Word of the Lord. Speak life over yourself, troubles don't last always.

Always remember that whatever season you're in, God is and will always be with you. *"When thou passest through the waters, I will be with thee; and through the rivers, they shall not overflow thee: when thou walkest through the fire, thou shalt not be burned; neither shall the flame kindle upon thee,"* (Isaiah 43:2). Sometimes, in our season of life, God will come to prove us. Fear not for God is come to prove you, and that His fear may be before your faces that you sin not (Ex. 20:20). Our lives and our forever changing seasons never stand still. Remember, God is the one who controls the times and the seasons in our lives. He's doing a Romans 8:28. Whatever season we're in, He's working it out for our good.

When He says it's a time to plant in our lives and a time to pluck up what is planted; it's a time to sow, and there is a time to harvest, reaping what you have sown. "Pluck up" is a season of weeding; getting something out that is not growing. Sometimes, we need to get rid of things in our lives that are keeping us from growing and one major thing is a lack of gratitude.

*'Make a joyful noise unto the LORD, all ye lands. Serve the LORD with gladness: come before His presence with singing. Know ye that the LORD He is God: it is He that hath made us, and not we ourselves; we are His people, and the sheep of His pasture. Enter into His gates with thanksgiving, and into His courts with praise: be thankful unto Him, and bless his name. For the LORD is good; His mercy is everlasting; and His truth endureth to all generations,'* Psalm 100:1-5.

As human beings that are somewhat 'prone' to being unholy and selfish, we will have children who we would move mountains for without blinking an eye. When a parent does certain things for their kids, their kids come to them happy and screaming 'thank you,' you can imagine the kind of joy that it would bring. All they care about and show to others in gratitude is, "oh, mom just got us a teddy bear to play with." One thing is sure; the next time that parent is coming home, there will be a nudge to do even more for those kids. That is what gratitude does, and that is just man. Human, sinful man. Then, there is God, your maker and my maker. How much more will He do?

Gratitude should not be tied to getting what you want. I think that comes from a place of entitlement and lack of contentment. Life has a way of increasing the standards, every single time you reach the one you thought was the highest. You start your high school education, and you can hardly wait to get the most beautiful grades. You get great grades, and you suddenly want to be the best basketball player on your team. You do that and next, you want to apply for that full scholarship to study at Yale. You struggle and struggle to get that sorted, and next, you want a job that will pay you six digits. That comes through and you want extra benefits from your job. The race never really ends, so at what point will you look back and see how far off you have really come? Are you really going to wait until it is *all* sorted before you acknowledge the hand of God in your life? That should not be, because it never really ends!

You may be so far off from where you want to be, but remember you are also very far from the beginning you had. It was not always this good, even if it is not the best right now. Now and again, God a way of reminding people to be grateful for their conditions in life, and He sometimes does this through tragedy, misfortune, or allowing us to visit those in hospice or hospital care. Take a day to go to the emergency ward in the hospital and see the people fighting for their lives in there. Just maybe you would be able to be thankful even in your 'down time.' Do you know how many people are praying and wishing to have something as 'good' as your downtime? That is because they are in worse times! God is teaching each of us different lessons, so we must learn to be thankful for all of it.

You should not be quick to look for the bad things in your life to complain about because believe me, there will always be bad things to point out. The people who seem to have the life you want, best believe they have problems too! No one has it all figured out so wherever you are at, be sure to be grateful!

Do not be all about hustling and struggling to get that 'perfect' life in the next few years. Take a break and look to God in Heaven to say, thank you for what you have. Watch the beauty of nature and the wonders of the work of God around you. Take a walk in the park and interact with people more often. Maybe then, you will find a couple of things to be thankful for. Let us look at a few benefits of gratitude:

1. Gratitude leaves you feeling happy. When you think of how far you come, you are happier because your progress is more apparent. You feel more satisfied with your current state in life, and this causes happiness and true joy. The way you see yourself improves! If you want to be happier in life, practice gratitude!

2. It can help you handle hard times better. Because hard times will always come, we need to learn how to go through them with a light heart and a heavy smile, not the other way around. Tell yourself that it will pass, because it will, and try to learn the lesson that life wants to teach you right there. When you are grateful, your mind does this thing where it seeks the good and tries to see more things to be grateful about. And yes, when you are grumpy and sad, your mind helps you find even more things to be sad about!

3. God will do more! God will move more mountains for you. The Bible says in Matthew 6:25-27, *'Therefore I tell you, do not worry about your life, what you will eat or drink; or about your body, what you will wear. Is not life more than food, and the body more than clothes? Look at the birds of the air; they do not sow or reap or store away in barns, and yet your heavenly Father feeds them. Are you not much more valuable than they? Can any one of you by worrying add a single hour to your life?'* When you worry, you are telling God that He is not doing a great job taking care of you. You are telling Him that even though He has control of your life, you would rather it your way, and He can take the back seat. Yet, when you are grateful and you express it in thanksgiving, you are telling God that everything He gives you is great, and you trust Him to keep caring for you all the days of your life.

Decide today to express gratitude to God and to the people around you, no matter what the circumstance is. *'Rejoice always, pray continually, give thanks in all circumstances; for this is God's will for you in Christ Jesus,'* 1 Thessalonians 5:16-18.

# Seasons

Dr. Brenda Jefferson

**CHAPTER THREE**

**TRUST GOD – UNDERSTANDING HIS POWER**

*'Trust in the LORD with all thine heart; and lean not unto thine own understanding. In all thy ways acknowledge him, and he shall direct thy paths. Be not wise in thine own eyes: fear the LORD, and depart from evil. It shall be health to thy navel, and marrow to thy bones,'* Proverbs 3:5-8.

With all that we have discussed thus far, we must see the importance of trusting God. It is just too important to be pushed aside. He knows and sees all things, so we must learn to put all of our trust in His wisdom, power, omnipotence, and guidance for us. As Christians, trusting in the Lord is an essential task. The first step toward trusting the Lord with all your heart is to accept His free gift of eternal life. To "trust in the Lord with all your heart" is possible because the Lord Himself has provided all the resources we need to be totally reliant upon Him.

Sometimes, we jump ahead of ourselves. We, humans, tend to be too quick at times, trying to find quick solutions so a problem does not fully surface or grow bigger than it is. The Bible warns us in

Psalm 32:9, saying; *'Be ye not as the horse, or as the mule, which have no understanding: whose mouth must be held in with bit and bridle, lest they come near unto thee.'* You see, the psalmist is trying to communicate an important principle. A mule, which is an offspring of a female mare, has to be incessantly prodded or nudged in order to make it budge. Being like a mule means that God has to force you to move by pulling your reins toward where He wants you to go. Whereas, a horse behaves quite the opposite. Here, God has to force us to halt by tightly pulling back the reins.

The problem with being like a horse is that when we get excited, we get way ahead of ourselves; as a result, we move in the flesh rather than in the Spirit. If we move impulsively in timing not ordained by God, we are entirely liable to make mistakes. As said in Proverbs 19:2, *"Enthusiasm without knowledge is no good; haste makes mistakes."* So, don't go about having that 'You only live once' attitude unless you want to 'burn your fingers,' as they say (which the devil will be very pleased about). In Ecclesiastes 3:1, King Solomon notes, *'For everything there is a season, a time to every purpose under Heaven.'* In Ecclesiastes 3:11, he continues, *'He hath made every thing beautiful in his time: also he hath set the world in their heart, so that no man can find out the work that God maketh from the beginning to the end.'* Only when something is done in God's perfect timing is it guaranteed to have splendid results. It is like baking a cookie. If you pull it out of the oven early, you have a raw batter – this is not good to eat. If you take it out late, you have a burnt-out snack – not good either. You will only have the perfect cookie when you pull it out of the oven at the right time. In the same way, we need to allow God to pull us out when His time is right. He is never late, He is always on time, just be patient and trust in Him. So, how do we learn to put our trust in God? How do we learn to silence the voice in our heads that tell us to take control of our lives, yanking it out of God's hands? Here are a few ways that we can put trust into practice, until it goes into the core of our very essence.

### 1. Never trust in your own understanding.

In the world we live in, we hear things like 'trust must be earned' when dealing with our human counterparts and we stand by such rules. If we choose to stand by this when dealing with things of God, we can tell that He has earned far more trust than we even have to give. King Solomon tells us that we must not lean on our own understanding. We may think we know too much but we can never really be wiser than the One who created us. The power of God is 'surreal,' and it can never disappoint us. You may have gone through some disappointment that make you feel like you need to build a high wall in your heart and show up for yourself when troubles arise. This is what the devil wants! The Bible says in Proverbs 18:1-2, *'Through desire a man, having separated himself, seeketh and intermeddleth with all wisdom. A fool hath no delight in understanding, but that his heart may discover itself.'* Is this what you choose to be? Definitely not. Open your heart to God and lay your trust down at His feet. He has all the wisdom that we may ever need to plunge ahead in life. Romans 11:33 reads *'O the depth of the riches both of the wisdom and knowledge of God! how unsearchable are his judgments, and his ways past finding out!'*

Yes, it may not be especially easy to trust Him completely, but we must learn to surrender.

## 2. Let God hear your heart's cry.

You know, sometimes we want something, but in all sincerity and with all our human effort, we are unable to get it. It is like someone who is so accustomed to hard labor and the usual hustle and bustle being told that they never have to toil for the rest of their lives, they can just sit at home and have their needs attended to. It will be extremely uncomfortable for that person! So yes, it can get difficult to put your trust in God when all you have known as help, was your own effort. The Bible says that in everything that we do, we should acknowledge Him, and He will make our way straight (Proverbs 3:6). Everything. So, speak to God about it. Tell Him what the matter is (even if the matter is your inability to trust in Him fully) and He will find a way out for you. Give the keys of your life to God and allow Him to take the wheel.

## 3. Put God first, every single day of your life.

It is almost natural for humans to want to put themselves first in everything they do. In spending, in celebrations, in accolades, and in encouragement, everyone wants to come first. But it is a wise man who will put God first. It is like walking down a dark and lonely road and you just skip into it, simply because you want to be first; this is foolishness. However, it is wise to place God ahead of everything else. It is saying to Him, 'Lord, I do not know the way that is right for me to go, so I trust you to lead me right till the very end and beyond.'

Even in your finance, *especially* in your finances. We tend to hold on to our money, procrastinate in paying tithes, and refuse to give offerings. I think the root cause for this is that we do not trust God to provide what we have, in a million-fold, so we find it hard to let go. Yes, that money is a central currency down here on Earth, but your trust in God is a divine and more powerful currency that will open doors that millions of dollars will never open.

### 4. Flee from evil.

The instruction is not to walk, crawl, or consider how bad the evil is before taking a step in the opposite direction. The instruction is to flee! There are so many different devices of the devil which are meant to destroy the working relationship between you and God. 1 John 2:15-17 says it all; *'Do not love the world or the things in the world. If anyone loves the world, the love of the Father is not in him. For all that is in the world – the lust of the flesh, the lust of the eyes, and the pride of life – is not of the Father but is of the world. And the world is passing away, and the lust of it; but he who does the will of God abides forever.'* Be diligent in your dealings. Remember, that all things that are good come from God, never from the devil. Flee from evil and live your life daily in pursuit of righteousness. This is the best way to live life. Protect your heart from the contaminations of the devil, that flies around the world. He will tell you that God has forsaken you, but you must know your truth and stand by it at all times.

### 5. Build a habit of reading the Word of God.

You know, something we need to be careful of as humans and as children of God is 'self-righteousness.' That is, you look at your actions, your deeds, and your way of life and you decide that you are righteous. That is not your duty to decide, and if we are not careful, this often leads to the onset of judgmental behavior towards others when they do things differently. The only yardstick that we must constantly use to check our lives is the Word of God.

The Word of God is our manual for living, and we must learn to stick by it. How do we learn to trust in God when we do not know what His Word says? It is almost impossible. Study God's promises daily and when you look at your life and see how much has been fulfilled, your trust in Him will grow.

### 6. Listen to the voice of the Holy Spirit.

The Holy Spirit is the Helper that was given to us by God. John 14:26 says, *'But the Helper, the Holy Spirit, whom the Father will send in My name, He will teach you all things, and bring to your remembrance all things that I said to you.'* With the Holy Spirit, you have the help you need in all your endeavors. You never have to worry about doing things by yourself. The Holy Spirit guides us into all truth and protects us from the devices of evil.

### 7. Rest in the love of God for you.

Sometimes, we easily doubt that God cares for us, especially when we come face-to-face with difficulties. We start asking questions like 'why do bad things happen to good people?' and 'where is God now that I need Him the most?' and so on. Listen, God never takes a break from caring for you and watching over you. You are His special creation and He sees everything that moves around you. Even in the midst of setbacks and trials, God stays by our side and helps us to learn from that experience to be better versions of ourselves. We no longer see these many obstacles as failures, but we see them as an opportunity to grow into what God wants us to be. Matthew 28:20 says, *'I am with you always, even to the end of the age.'* We must learn to trust God! No, it is not easy, but daily, get rid of your flesh and pick up strength in your spirit from the Almighty God, knowing that you are not alone.

**Rejoice in God.**

*'Be kindly affectioned one to another with brotherly love; in honour preferring one another; Not slothful in business; fervent in spirit; serving the Lord; Rejoicing in hope; patient in tribulation; continuing instant in prayer,'* Romans 12:10-12.

Throughout the sufferings of Apostle Paul, one thing was sure; He was joyful! Philippians 3:1 says, 'Finally, my brethren, rejoice in the Lord. For me to write the same things to you *is* not tedious, but for you *it is* safe.' He is glad and urges us to be the same. Paul talks about his joy many times, even when he was in prison! Throughout the span of his letters, he urges his brothers and sisters, you and me, to rejoice in the Lord and be glad. Clearly, it was extremely important. It must have been extremely difficult, almost impossible! But it is worthy of emulating. So we must ask, how can one live this type of life? How do you intentionally build up joy in your spirit and in your heart, so that your growth is a delight to God and your life pleases Him? There are a couple of ways; we will call them the Ways of Joy. Let us look at these ways in context and see how to please God by altering the states of our hearts.

**Abiding in God, and God in you.** John 15:1-8 says, *'I am the true vine, and my Father is the husbandman. Every branch in Me that beareth not fruit He taketh away: and every branch that beareth fruit, He purgeth it, that it may bring forth more fruit. Now ye are clean through the word which I have spoken unto you. Abide in Me,* *and I in you. As the branch cannot bear fruit of itself, except it abide in the vine; no more can ye, except ye abide in Me. I am the vine, ye are the branches: He that abideth in Me, and I in him, the same bringeth forth much fruit: for without Me ye can do nothing. If a man abide not in Me, he is cast forth as a branch, and is withered; and men gather them, and cast them into the fire, and they are burned. If ye abide in Me, and my words abide in you, ye shall ask what ye will, and it shall be done unto you. Herein is my Father glorified, that ye bear much fruit; so shall ye be my disciples.'* The following verses allow us to see that if we keep the commandments of God, we will abide in love. It says in verses 9-11 'As the Father loved Me, I also have loved you; abide in My love. If you keep My commandments, you will abide in My love, just as I have kept My Father's commandments and abide in His love.' These things I have spoken to you, that My joy may remain in you, and *that* your joy may be full. This is My commandment, that you love one another as I have loved you.'

Now, it has shown us again, the important relationship between communion and our dwelling in Christ Jesus. That is to say, for your joy to be full, you have to be in a continuous and intentional relationship with Christ Jesus, a working relationship. When we pray and carry out a couple of other different spiritual exercises, we strengthen our relationship with God. The more you move in Christ, living closer to Him, the more your joy grows. We must abide in Christ.

**Believing.** Romans 15:13 says, *'Now may the God of hope fill you with all joy and peace in believing, that you may abound in hope by the power of the Holy Spirit.'* Our faith in God gives us joy! So, in order to have a life filled with the joy of the Lord, we must put our trust in Him. You have to believe that everything He plans for you is best and comes from a place of love. You also have to believe in His Word and trust in the power of potency of it. Peter writes to Christians who are suffering and says the same thing to them, *'Though you have not seen Him, you love Him. Though you do not now see Him, you believe in Him and rejoice with joy that is not expressible and is filled with glory.'* Simply by placing your belief in Him, you bring joy into your heart.

**Meditating.** The scripture component of meditating on the Word of God is dependent on us not just reading, putting that Word on the inside of us. Remember the psalmist in Psalm 1:2 *"His delight is in the law of the Lord, and on his law, he meditates day and night."* Or take Psalm 19:8, *"The precepts of the Lord are right, rejoicing the heart."* God's Word makes our hearts glad. Let us take a quick glance at Psalm 119 and see how frequently it speaks of rejoicing and joy. Verse 16 says, *"I will delight in your statutes; I will not forget your Word."* Verse 111 says, *"Your testimonies are my heritage forever, for they are the joy of my heart."* Verse 162 says, *"I rejoice at your Word like one who finds great spoil."* Meditating on the Word is a key to heartfelt rejoicing.

If you want to be happy in the Lord, you are going to have to be in the Word of God. You're going to have to be reading it, you're going to have to be meditating on it, and you're going to have to be delighting in Him. In fact, even the way Paul phrases this first verse shows us this. He says, "Finally, my brothers, rejoice in the Lord.

To write the same things to you is no trouble to me and is safe for you."

He is reminding them of certain things. He is going over the same things again and again. Why is he doing it? It is safe for them, he says. He is going to go on and talk about other aspects of this, including a warning that we'll look at next week, but one reason he is writing what he writes is for them to rejoice. Truth leads to joy. The Word of God leads to joy.

**Repenting.** There is a crucial place for repentance in the life of the Christian. In fact, Martin Luther said, "The whole life of the Christian is to be one of repentance." What is repentance? Well, repentance is turning from sin, and sin is the great blocker of joy. In fact, if you were to say that the presence of Christ is the oxygen for joy, sin is the opposite. Sin is a poisonous gas. It just chokes the life out of happiness.

You might think of sin as the joy killers in your life, the joy substitutes, the things that get in the way of real joy. The greatest unhappiness in your life at this moment is due to sin. I have found by experience, as I'm sure many of you have as well, that when I find myself on a downward spiral into old sin patterns, I can almost always trace it back to a lack of delighting in the Lord, a lack of fellowship with God, and a lack of time with Him. The way back is repentance.

*Do you remember David, in Psalm 51?* He wrote this wonderful psalm after his repentance from committing adultery with Bathsheba. One of the things he says in Psalm 51 is, 'Restore to me the joy of your salvation, and uphold me with a willing spirit.' If joy is lacking in your life this morning, maybe one thing you need to do is some self-examination, and ask, "Where have you broken fellowship with God, and where is repentance needed?" Then turn from sin and turn to Christ.

The fifth way of joy would be gratitude, thanking God. That would include gratitude for both the big blessings of salvation, but also gratitude for the little things, the ordinary blessings of life, and even what we might call the "seasons of trials.' It is only right for us to rejoice in the Lord in those things, to thank God for those things, and let that lead us to deeper joy in Him.

The psalmist understood this in Psalm 104:14-15. 'You cause the grass to grow for the livestock, and plants for man to cultivate, that he may bring forth food from the Earth and wine to gladden the heart of man, oil to make his face shine, and bread to strengthen man's heart.'

Now, here's this psalmist living in the ancient world, and he's looking at just some of the staples of life for the person in the time period. He is saying that God gave these things to gladden the heart of man, to give him strength. I think you could say of every innocent pleasure, of every created good, of every blessing that genuinely comes to us from the hand of God, that it is right for us to be glad for them, as long as we can thank God for them and we can then let those pleasures lead us back to God, the great giver of all blessings.

Finally, hoping in the Lord, and especially hoping in what is yet to come. Even in the midst of our suffering, we are looking ahead to what God is yet to do.

Let's reflect on Romans Chapter 5. Paul says, "Through Him, we have also obtained access by faith into this grace in which we stand, and we rejoice in hope of the glory of God. Not only that, but we rejoice in our sufferings..." Take note here, we rejoice in hope, we rejoice in our sufferings, "knowing that suffering produces endurance, endurance produces character, character produces hope, and hope does not put us to shame, because the love of God has been poured into our hearts through the Holy Spirit who has been given to us."

In other words, even in the midst of suffering, we are looking ahead, we're looking to the future, we are looking to the new world that God will create, the new Heavens and the new Earth when Jesus comes again, and He makes all things new. That is a source of joy. That is a means, a way of cultivating joy in the Lord.

**All of these ways - abiding, believing, meditating, repenting, thanking God, hoping in the Lord – all of these are ways to cultivate joy in our lives.** Let me just ask you in this moment, what is your happiness level? What is your joy level? Think about your basic disposition and your basic attitude over the last few days. *Have you been rejoicing in the Lord, rather than moaning and groaning and complaining? Are you happy as a person? Are you satisfied with God?*

## Dr. Brenda Jefferson

Let us pray.

*Our gracious, merciful God, we thank you for your word. We thank you for the possibility of joy, of such deep joy that your word commends to us, that it holds out to us. We thank you for the challenge of your word. This is a challenging passage for us because it forces us to examine our hearts and to ask what the source of our happiness is, and what we depend on. We thank you for the hope that is in your word, that even we who have so often not rejoiced in you can, through the power of your Spirit, find joy in Jesus Christ. I pray that that would be the case this morning. Father, as we come to the Lord's Table, may it be a time of renewed fellowship with the Lord Jesus. May we learn to live in union and in communion with him, with our eyes set on you and on your word, believing your promises, hoping in your mercy. So, draw near to us in these moments as we draw near to you, minister to us by your Spirit, we pray in Jesus' name and for His sake, Amen.*

Seasons

Dr. Brenda Jefferson

# 30-Day DEVOTIONAL

# 30-Days of Devotion

| Purpose | Prayer | Description |
|---|---|---|
| | | |
| | | |
| | | |
| | | |
| | | |

| 1. | 2. | 3. | 4. | 5. | 6. | 7. | 8. | 9. | 10 |
|---|---|---|---|---|---|---|---|---|---|
| 11. | 12. | 13. | 14. | 15. | 16. | 17. | 18. | 19. | 20 |
| 21. | 22. | 23. | 24. | 25. | 26. | 27. | 28. | 29. | 30 |

Dr. Brenda Jefferson

# PART ONE: SEASON IN, SEASON OUT

## DAY ONE:

### A FATHER'S LOVE

***Bible verse:*** *'No, in all these things we are more than conquerors through him who loved us. For I am convinced that neither death nor life, neither angels nor demons, neither the present nor the future, nor any powers, neither height nor depth, nor anything else in all creation, will be able to separate us from the love of God that is in Christ Jesus our Lord,'* Romans 8:37-39.

One morning, Josh got into a bad fight at school. Another boy from his class tried to pick at him in the cafeteria and Josh would just not have it. He hit him in the face a couple of times and before he could shake the anger away, the boy had blood running from his nostrils and a black eye. As expected, Josh was punished severely and made to do service within the school premises for two weeks. Josh could not tell his dad about this, he knew that he would be very disappointed by it. He took a long walk home each day because the bus would have left by the time he was done and had to put up a big smile when he got home so no one would sense what was wrong.

One afternoon, it was really hot, and Josh got home smelly and tired. He was about to put up his same act when his father asked randomly, and Josh told him the entire truth with shaky fingers and his head bent toward the ground. To his utmost surprise, his dad burst out laughing and gave him a tap on the shoulder. "I know you would not do that if you were not very pissed, but I am also glad that you are learning your lesson."

Josh was more than sorry, and also awfully glad that he had not disappointed his dad. After that afternoon, Josh's Dad offered to pick Josh up every day after school, and his mom agreed to give him a nice treat of cookies and ice cream for every day he worked.


How much more God? The love that God has for you and me cannot be completely understood; we can't entirely wrap our minds around it. It's so good that it feels unreal. When we are in our darkest times, the devil wants us to think that we have been forsaken by God, but the opposite is always the case. If you have a kid or any dependent, take some time to think about it! The little one gets into some trouble, is ill, can't find their way around something, etc. Would that be the time you leave, or would that be the time you show how much you care?

You have the answer!


**Confession:** I know that I am loved by God. In my down times, God is present, and He is taking care of me. In my state of confusion, He is standing by me all the way.

**Prayer:** Almighty Father, thank you for the gift of your love. Thank you for your care and your protection in every phase of my life. I pray that you open my eyes to see your hand in my situations, even when it does not feel like it, and when it seems like there is no hope. Amen.

## DAY TWO:

### GOD IS GOD, NOT A MAN

**Bible verse:** *'God is not a man, that He should lie, nor a son of man, that He should repent. Has He said, and will He not do? Or has He spoken, and will He not make it good?'* Numbers 23:19.

Many things are typical of us as humans. That is, there are certain things that we would do simply because we are human, and it is how we are wired. If we look at the biological makeup, we will see that there is an area in the brain that is stimulated by light so that we wake up when the day gets bright and feel sleepy when it gets darker. If we look at the mental and emotional make-ups, there are also some things that are the way they are just because we are human.

A lion would see a smaller animal and jump at it for lunch because it is carnivorous, and a snail would crawl to a nice green leaf and nibble on it for lunch. Nothing we do or do not do will make a lion eat grass, or make a snail eat meat. If anything, it would involve scientific variations and if it is successful, then the animal can no longer be referred to as a lion or a snail. It simply is not in the nature of any of those animals to eat what they cannot eat.

This is the same way it is with God. The Bible tells us about the Holiness of God and how sin is not in His nature. When we deal with humans, we expect to hear lies, get cheated or abandoned, and get mixed up with a lot of drama, yes, because we are dealing with humans. However, it would be silly of us to think the same of God because none of those are in His nature. 1 John 1:5 says *'This is the message we have heard from him and proclaim to you, that God is light, and in him is no darkness at all.'* There is no fault in the being of God.

What does this mean for you and me? It means that when God says that He will do a thing, He most certainly will! He would not say that He loves you and proceed to treat you without love.

It is just not who He is!

**Confession:** Today, I align my spirit with the realness of God. I align my heart to the nature of God, and I begin to trust in His Word and will for me, no matter what the world says.

**Prayer:** Thank you for your word today, Lord. Thank you for showing your true nature to me and helping me see you for who you are. I pray that from this day onward, I am not swirled by the uncertainties of the world but held fast by the truth in your Word.

# DAY THREE:

## DYING DAILY

***Bible verse:*** *'What shall we say then? Shall we continue in sin that grace may abound? Certainly not! How shall we who died to sin live any longer in it? Or do you not know that as many of us as were baptized into Christ Jesus were baptized into His death? Therefore we were buried with Him through baptism into death, that just as Christ was raised from the dead by the glory of the Father, even so we also should walk in newness of life,'* Romans 6:1-4.

You and I are spirit and flesh. Here on earth, one cannot exist without the other seeing that the spirit lives in the flesh and the flesh lives 'on' the spirit. This is not a problem physically, but you and I know that the matters of life are more than the eyes can see. The Bible says in Matthew 26:41, *'Watch and pray, lest you enter into temptation. The spirit indeed is willing, but the flesh is weak.'* In many other parts of the Bible, we see warnings about how the flesh is capable of pulling the Spirit into a place of eternal damnation. Ever wondered why? It is because the flesh has the power to pull the Spirit, **only** when the Spirit is not strong enough to pull in the other direction.

The flesh wants what it wants. Untamed and untrained, it lusts after the things of life and seeks to displease God. The flesh is powerful enough to cause a huge rift between us (our spirits) and the Spirit of God.

So, what is a way out of this trouble? To die daily.

When we look at the life of Paul, it is easy to wonder what driving force he had. Why would a man be beaten and persecuted but preach still? Why would a man be locked up behind bars in a prison cell and still give God praise? The answer is that he practiced dying daily.

Dying daily is constantly taking power away from your flesh and handing it over to your spirit. It is telling your flesh that it has no say over your actions, and it will only do as the Spirit says.

Dying daily is letting go of the desires of the flesh and focusing on the will of God. This is the true way that God wants you and me to live.

**Confession:** I declare that every hold of lust and sin in me is broken today. I do the Lord's work here on Earth, and my spirit is constantly aligned with the will of God.

**Prayer:** Lord, I come to you today to ask for help with letting go of my flesh. I want to live a life that pleases you, and I do not want to go against your commandments. Give me the strength that I need to overcome. In Jesus' name, Amen.

## DAY FOUR:

### DYING DAILY #2

***Bible verse:*** *'If your right eye causes you to sin, pluck it out and cast it from you; for it is more profitable for you that one of your members perish, than for your whole body to be cast into hell,'* Matthew 5:29.

So, now we know what it means to die daily. But how do we do that? What must we learn to do in order to reduce the power the flesh has over the Spirit?

One thing is certain; the Spirit has to get stronger! It has to learn how to put the flesh in its place, as inferior. Why? Because the flesh is not following the spirit to eternity.

Listen, when we die, our flesh stays down here and the Spirit faces judgment. Whichever side of eternity that the spirit ends up on is for the spirit alone, and the flesh does not get to experience it. Think about this the next time the lust of the flesh tries to lure your spirit into turning away from God. Imagine it as a 'bad friend' who wants to try putting you in a mess or predicament, that it would not willingly experience with you.

The Bible, in its knowledge and wisdom explains this. It tells us to pluck out the right eye, if that is what causes us to sin. No, this is not only literal. It means anything at all that causes you to deviate from the will of God, simply needs to go! It could be friends, it could be work, environment, lifestyle choices, family, or anything at all! It just needs to go because nothing is worth losing your salvation for. What benefit is it for us to gain and enjoy the pleasures of this life, and lose our soul.

While it's easier said than done, to stay in a box or closed room to prevent trouble, or bad decisions. In reality, you have to train your spirit to have the upper say. Feed your spirit with life and watch it grow in strength. Where do we find life? In the Word of God.

Form a habit of running to God for guidance, because what better place is there to go than to the one who created life itself?

As we close this day's devotion, I want to urge you to be sure of your stance. Do not be quick to make decisions, be intentional about your walk with God. It will not always be easy, especially when in difficult seasons, but God's word stands.

**Confession:** I am not a slave to sin and to the lust of the flesh. I have victory over sin, and I am aligned with the will of God in my life.

**Prayer:** Today, I pray for the strength to overcome sin, temptation, confusion, and disobedience. I pray that no matter what situation I find myself in, I will hold on to God and never turn my back on Him in search of faster routes. Amen.

# DAY FIVE:

## THE TEN VIRGINS

***Bible verse:*** *'And the foolish said to the wise, 'Give us some of your oil, for our lamps are going out.' But the wise answered, saying, 'No, lest there should not be enough for us and you; but go rather to those who sell, and buy for yourselves.' And while they went to buy, the bridegroom came, and those who were ready went in with him to the wedding; and the door was shut.'* Matthew 25:8-10.

Many of us know about the story of the ten virgins in the Bible. It was quite a sad one the first time I heard it because I really wished that the 'foolish' made it in time, but I guess there will always be consequences for actions, right?

Yes, and there will also be consequences for inaction too! If you read the beginning of the chapter, you would see that these ten virgins all had one thing in common, and that was the expected end. It is just like a young child being told he would receive a brand-new video game on his fifth birthday. That will continue to linger in the boy's mind until that promise is met and the video game is really given to him. These ten virgins were to meet with the bridegroom and I am pretty sure they waited and dreamt of the day, for as long as they could. Now, out of the ten, five were not just dreaming about that glorious day, they were also planning about it. They were asking themselves questions like 'what could go wrong? How do I go about this if it comes up? But on the other hand, the other five were only fantasizing about the glorious day, filled with excitement, and doing nothing to plan towards it.

Of course, we can assume that the situation they were in at the time was very terrible, and hearing that they would be meeting with the bridegroom made them so eager, but did it yield well? Of course not.

We must know that every situation we find ourselves in is very significant, and its use can never be rolled over without consequences. The foolish virgins were so eager for their time to party, that they made no good use of their sober time. As a consequence, they lost their chance to party.

We must be very careful when it comes to the things of life. Take your time to discern the season you are in and use it well. A saying I heard once goes, 'To find a black goat, you need to search during the day, not at night' and that goes well to tell us how important it is that we discern what time is day and what time is night. You should always order your goals and follow them before it's too late to accomplish them.

**Confession:** I do not get my timing wrong. At the right time, I will be at the right place and doing the right things only. I will not make costly mistakes, that will cost me the next seasons of my life.

**Prayer:** Lord, I pray that you open my eyes and my heart to wisdom. I pray that you guide me to do what is right, at the right time, so I do not get it wrong in life. Amen.

## DAY SIX:

### CURSE GOD AND DIE

**Bible verse:** *'Then his wife said to him, "Do you still hold fast to your integrity? Curse God and die!'* Job 2:9.

If you take some good time to read the book of Job, maybe you would understand the stance of the person that made the statement 'Curse God and die'. Job literally went from 1000 to zero in a very short period of time. Cursing God was like committing suicide, but maybe if we could rank people that had enough reasons to commit suicide, Job would probably rank top ten. Imagine how empty he would have felt from once having it all - riches, cattle, mansions, lands, and so much more - to having nothing at all.

His own wife looked at him and saw that there was no hope for him, and she decided that it was better for him to die than to live because he had been 'forsaken' by God.

But that is the voice of the devil, not the voice of God. When we find ourselves in tight and difficult situations, the devil tries to tell us to turn our backs on the one solution to our problem. He makes God look bad, whispers all sorts into our ears, and gives us ideas that we have to figure out by ourselves because God is not present but that is untrue.

In your lowest times, you need to run to God, not away from God. You must know that if you lose everything in life, and all you have is God by your side, you have all that you will ever need.

This is why the Bible tells us many times to seek the Kingdom of God first and have everything else added.

Job did not curse God, and he certainly did not die. He had his feet planted in God and he trusted God even till the last point. His own health was failing, and his skin was filled with boils. He did not let go of the faithfulness of God.

So, ask yourself, do you have all of your trust in God? Do you know for a fact that God can never and will never forsake you, no matter how bad it gets?

**Confession:** I am a child of God, and as such, God will never forsake me. As long as I live, I choose to put my hope in God and in his power. No power says no if God says yes in my life.

**Prayer:** Father, I want to rest in you. I want to be able to believe in all that you have said in our words concerning me no matter where I find myself. Teach me to have undying and unshaken faith in you. Lead me aright, so the devil is unable to pull me away from you. In Jesus' name, Amen.

## DAY SEVEN:

### PEACE, BE STILL

**Bible verse:** *'Peace I leave with you, my peace I give to you; not as the world gives do I give to you. Let not your heart be troubled, neither let it be afraid,'* John 14:27.

In your life (and mine as well), things will get hard and tough. We know for a fact that we will come face to face with encounters that can leave us drained and wondering about the essence of life. Many times, things get so back in such a consecutive and persistent manner, it almost feels like the devil himself decided to take something out on you. This is not new under the sun and also not unique to only you.

When Jesus came to earth as flesh and blood, he spent many of his days on earth healing people of diseases and sicknesses, preaching life, and solving people's problems. So yes, there have always been things to fix, even for the people who lived in the same city as the Savior, Jesus Christ. Let us come further and look at the lives of the disciples of Jesus Christ. They were not excluded from sufferings simply because they followed Jesus Christ around doing the will of the Father. Even Jesus Himself was not excluded from it. They all faced various levels of temptations, persecutions, and real-life issues. They had day-to-day matters arising, and in the middle of it all, they followed Jesus. The Bible says in Mark 4:35-41 *'On the same day, when evening had come, He said to them, "Let us cross over to the other side." Now when they had left the multitude, they took*

*Him along in the boat as He was. And other little boats were also with Him. And a great windstorm arose, and the waves beat into the boat, so that it was already filling. But He was in the stern, asleep on a pillow. And they awoke Him and said to Him, "Teacher, do You not care that we are perishing?" Then He arose and rebuked the wind, and said to the sea, "Peace, be still!" And the wind ceased and there was a great calm. But He said to them, "Why are you so fearful? How is it that you have no faith?" And they feared exceedingly, and said to one another, "Who can this be, that even the wind and the sea obey Him!"*

This part of the Bible says so much to us and questions the level of our faith in Christ. Each time I hear it, I ask myself, 'how could these disciples, even after seeing the power of Jesus Christ firsthand so many times still choose to fear their fate in the middle of a violent storm? But really and truly, I can't say that I would have done any better!

God is telling you today to trust him, to let go of your weak feelings and grow your faith in Him. In the midst of your fears, confusion, and pains, it may look as though He does not care for you, or that He is silent and absent, but that is not the truth. Through it all, God is by your side. He knows what you are experiencing. He knows what your problems are and He is asking you to maintain a state of calm and quiet. He is saying to those problems and difficulties 'be still!'

Your response to problems should not be to panic. Panicking shows a low level of faith and an extent of distrust in the power of God. Panicking, is you trying to solve the problem by any means possible, not wanting to leave it in the hands of God. That is not what God wants you to respond with. Your response to problems should be 'peace, be still.' God wants you to know that He is by your side and has complete control of the situation. What do you say to Him today?

**Confession:** My God does not have a blind spot; He sees it all. In my tough times, He is by my side, giving me a soft landing. In all of my encounters, the Lord remains the King of my life, granting me peace and safety always.

**Prayer:** Father in Heaven, you see all things. Thank you for saving me always, for helping me, and for easing my pains. I pray today that anything that comes into my life and causes me to lose my faith and trust in you may be destroyed. May it be terminated and sent to the pit of hell, in Jesus' name. Amen.

## DAY EIGHT:

### NOT YOUR CROSS TO BEAR

***Bible verse:*** *'And He strictly warned and commanded them to tell this to no one, saying, "The Son of Man must suffer many things, and be rejected by the elders and chief priests and scribes, and be killed, and be raised the third day." Then He said to them all, "If anyone desires to come after Me, let him deny himself, and take up his cross daily, and follow Me,'* Luke 9:21-23.

When you first read or heard the words of Jesus that said, 'take up His cross daily,' what did you think? Did you think to yourself 'oh, I am on my own and faced with the problems of life?" or "my problems are not for Jesus to solve or help handle, but all mine to fix?" Let us look a bit at the part of the Bible that talks about bearing your cross.

**Luke 9:23-27 reads:**

*Then He said to them all, "If anyone desires to come after Me, let him deny himself, and take up his cross daily, and follow Me. For whoever desires to save his life will lose it, but whoever loses his life for My sake will save it. For what profit is it to a man if he gains the whole world, and is himself destroyed or lost? For whoever is ashamed of Me and My words, of him the Son of Man will be ashamed when He comes in His own glory, and in His Father's, and of the holy angels. But I tell you truly, there are some standing here who shall not taste death till they see the kingdom of God."*

Jesus was saying to His disciples that to follow Him, they would have to prepare their minds for the many trials and tribulations that will come their way for the cause. He tells them that in summary that it would not be a bed of roses walking the walk with Him. Because of this, some Christians have normalized and personalized suffering so much that they want to handle it all by themselves because they are *taking up their cross and walking with Jesus.* But there is a twist to this. Come with me.

At the same time, Matthew 11:28-30 says, *'Come to Me, all you who labor and are heavy laden, and I will give you rest. Take My yoke upon you and learn from Me, for I am gentle and lowly in heart, and you will find rest for your souls. For My yoke is easy and My burden is light.'* Your trials right now are expected, but that does not mean that you have to keep it all to yourself! We have a father that truly cares about us and about the way we feel. He does not want you to handle all of your problems by yourself. He wants you to come to Him so that he can give you rest!

Will you trust Him enough to do that today?

**Confession:** I am helped by God. When the going gets tough, I have a father that I can always lean on. I have the assistance and guidance that I need to live a life that is easy and blessed. I have God on my side!

**Prayer:** Thank you Lord Jesus for your word. Thank you for letting me know that you are with me even when I am bearing my cross. Thank you for making my matters the top of your list and thank you for taking care of me. In Jesus' name, Amen.

# DAY NINE:

## GUIDING YOU SAFELY

**Bible verse:** *'The steps of a good man are ordered by the Lord, and He delights in his way. Though he fall, he shall not be utterly cast down; for the Lord upholds him with His hand. I have been young, and now am old; yet I have not seen the righteous forsaken, nor his descendants begging bread. He is ever merciful and lends; and his descendants are blessed,'* Psalms 37:23-26.

When you have the Lord by your side, your steps are ordered and you have the higher advantage, the upper hand, over those who do not have Him. Imagine you are playing some game and you get to decide how things end up for the little characters down there. You know how it is going to go, so you do have an upper hand over the characters. If they happen to have a 'relationship' with you, you would tell them what their fate is and how they can prevent it or walk directly into it.

That is what it feels like with God. Proverbs 15:3 says, *'The eyes of the Lord are in every place, keeping watch on the evil and the good.'* Nothing happens here on the earth that the Lord does not see. Nothing at all is hidden from his sight. When we commit to the guidance of the Lord in our lives, the blessings that follow are extreme, and consistent too!

1. We have a companion forever. Joshua 1:9 says *'Have I not commanded you? Be strong and of good courage; do not be*

*afraid, nor be dismayed, for the Lord your God is with you wherever you go.'* No matter what your situation is, God will not change from the loving and present father that He is. He will remain with us.

2. We begin to experience rest. *'And He said, "My Presence will go with you, and I will give you rest."'* Exodus 33:14. This verse shows us that while we are still at it, on the way, God will give us rest. We would not have to wait till the end of the journey before we can heave a sigh of relief, He will give it to us as we go. So, we have calm and peace when we allow the Lord to guide our steps.

3. Our lives will be set apart from those without the guidance of God. Exodus 33:15-16 says, *'Then he said to Him, "If Your Presence does not go with us, do not bring us up from here. For how then will it be known that Your people and I have found grace in Your sight, except You go with us? So we shall be separate, Your people and I, from all the people who are upon the face of the earth."'* His presence and guidance makes all the difference. We are different when God's company goes with us because of the work that it does in us and through us.

4. The Lord will know us. Exodus 33:17 says *'So the Lord said to Moses, "I will also do this thing that you have spoken; for you have found grace in My sight, and I know you by name."'* If the president of the country or an extremely important person who you look up to knows you by name, you feel extremely important because that

makes all the difference that there is. So, if the maker of Heaven and earth knows you by name, it means everything is made whole.

As you agree to go with the guidance of the Lord in your life, you will experience each of these blessings and even more. It just will not be missed.

**Confessions:** I am under the care of the Lord most High. I have everything that I need, and He guides me safely through the way. I am protected, I am loved, and I am led right by the Lord, most High.

**Prayer:** Dear heavenly Father, thank you for your protection, guidance, and help. I pray that you give me the grace to abandon myself and my worries in your care. I trust you, and I hope to do this forever. Amen.

Dr. Brenda Jefferson

# DAY TEN:

## THE MERCY OF GOD

***Bible verse:*** *'If any of you lacks wisdom, let him ask of God, who gives to all liberally and without reproach, and it will be given to him. (5) But let him ask in faith, with no doubting, for he who doubts is like a wave of the sea driven and tossed by the wind. (7) For let not that man suppose that he will receive anything from the Lord; (8) he is a double-minded man, unstable in all his ways.'* James 1:5-8.

When Jesus met the first four disciples by the side of the river, they were working, right? Matthew 4:18-22 says, *'And Jesus, walking by the Sea of Galilee, saw two brothers, Simon called Peter, and Andrew his brother, casting a net into the sea; for they were fishermen. Then He said to them, "Follow Me, and I will make you fishers of men." They immediately left their nets and followed Him. Going on from there, He saw two other brothers, James the son of Zebedee, and John his brother, in the boat with Zebedee their father, mending their nets. He called them, and immediately they left the boat and their father, and followed Him.*

These men had families to feed (and this is why they were fishermen of fish) when Jesus met them at the river and asked them to follow Him. They did not look at him with disdain and say things like 'don't you know we have more important work to do?' or 'can you not see that we are working to make a living? We will come with you when we are less busy!' They said none of that. They knew that the work they had with Jesus was more important than whatever troubles they were going through so they stayed with that idea.

As merciful as the Lord is, they got to win on both ends. John 21:5-11 says, *'Then Jesus said to them, "Children, have you any food?" They answered Him, "No." And He said to them, "Cast the net on the right side of the boat, and you will find some." So they cast, and now they were not able to draw it in because of the multitude of fish. Therefore that disciple whom Jesus loved said to Peter, "It is the Lord!" Now when Simon Peter heard that it was the Lord, he put on his outer garment (for he had removed it) and plunged into the sea. But the other disciples came in the little boat (for they were not far from land, but about two hundred cubits), dragging the net with fish. Then, as soon as they had come to land, they saw a fire of coals there, and fish laid on it, and bread. Jesus said to them, "Bring some of the fish which you have just caught." Simon Peter went up and dragged the net to land, full of large fish, one hundred and fifty-three; and although there were so many, the net was not broken.'*

When you walk with Christ, you never fail. You win on all ends. On the flip side, when you choose to focus on your worries, fears, and problems, you will not be able to focus on God and sadly, you will not be able to sort that problem either.

*What is your choice today?*


**Confession:** I am not so overwhelmed by the troubles of life that I remove my focus from the Lord and the things He requires of me.

My heart is placed in the hands of God, and it stays there, no matter what my situation in life is.

**Prayer:** Dear Jesus, please help me to follow you without doubt and fear. Help me to shut out the pain of the world and focus my heart on you. In Jesus' name I pray, Amen.

# Seasons

## PART TWO: JESUS, OUR HOPE IN AGES PAST.

## DAY ELEVEN:

### THE GIFT THAT KEEPS GIVING

***Bible verse:*** *'For God so loved the world that He gave His only begotten Son, that whoever believes in Him should not perish but have everlasting life. For God did not send His Son into the world to condemn the world, but that the world through Him might be saved. "He who believes in Him is not condemned; but he who does not believe is condemned already, because he has not believed in the name of the only begotten Son of God,'* John 3:16-18.

As Christians, there is one thing that we must know. That many years ago, sin came into the world through one man, Adam. When that happened, the devil got a hold of the heart of man and sin became ingrained in the nature of man. A significant part of the foundation of the Christian faith is a sacrifice made by God the Father and God the Son many years ago. The story of the first man on earth in Genesis tells us about how sin entered the world, and God did many things to separate the bad ones, condemn them and let the good ones live. He destroyed Sodom and Gomorrah, and He also sent a great flood during the days of Noah to clear out the disobedient ones. But He saw that as sin came into the world through one man, then it will only leave through another man, and

He gave no one else as a sacrifice for the sins of the world but His Son, Jesus Christ.

Jesus Christ was born of the Holy Spirit and not a man. This not only makes Him pure but also Holy, as He knows no sin. The Bible teaches us in John 14:6 saying, *'Jesus said to him, "I am the way, the truth, and the life. No one comes to the Father except through Me.'* He came to us as a path, a redeeming path so that as many people who genuinely want to be saved can go in that direction and be saved, wholly and completely.

He is the gift that keeps giving.

But we must know that this gift is not an automatic gift that is given to all. John 3:16 allows us to know that there is a prerequisite, and that is 'faith.' A person who wishes to receive eternal life must believe in the sacrifice of Christ and must accept and acknowledge that indeed, while they were sinners, Christ died for them so that they may be free. There is no other way! Many may feel that just by being a good person, giving alms, and being kind to fellow man, you have an automatic ticket to the Kingdom of God, but that is not what the Bible teaches us. It says that Jesus Christ is the only way to go.

Accepting this gift is all that a man needs to be saved from the slavery that the devil unleashes on the world daily. This is a gift that makes all the difference.

Will you be accepting it today?

**Confession:** I believe that Jesus Christ died for my sins on the Cross of Cavalry. I accept today that He is the only way, and through the price that He has paid, I am now set free from the bondage of sin. I have eternal life in me through Christ Jesus. I AM FREE!

**Prayer:** Dear Lord Jesus, thank you for your kindness towards me. Thank you for even when I was not formed, you thought of me, and you paid the price for me. I declare that my faith in you is forever, and for this, eternal life is sure. Amen.

# DAY TWELVE:

## DESIRABLE TRANSFORMATION

***Bible verse:*** *'I beseech you therefore, brethren, by the mercies of God, that you present your bodies a living sacrifice, holy, acceptable to God, which is your reasonable service. And do not be conformed to this world, but be transformed by the renewing of your mind, that you may prove what is that good and acceptable and perfect will of God,'* Romans 12:1-2.

No one is made or born ready. No one is born perfect, sorted, and cleared free from the many troubles that come with life. We have been called to constantly work on our bodies, souls, and spirits until we are seen as pure and Holy by the Lord Himself. The second verse quoted above is something very important that we must always bear in our hearts as children of God.

The Bible teaches us that really and truly, poor or bad communication will always affect good morals negatively. Sadly, the world we live in is filled with such bad influences at alarming rates. We see bad people all around us or good people who have been affected negatively or who have allowed the devil to influence their choice of a lifestyle, and they somehow become his worker, pulling more people into that same hold. It is our sole duty as Christians and children of God to constantly renew our minds.

When we go to our places of work, school, or even in our neighborhoods, we can encounter people who may seem genuine but may have slipped just a little, and this can have ripple effects when we keep constant communication with them *without renewing our minds on a regular basis.*

The Lord wants us to mirror his will and desires to the world at all times. He wants us to tell the world what it really is to be a follower of Christ. We are more like ambassadors of Heaven here on earth, and truth is, it is a full-time role. We can never be caught off guard doing the wrong things. To achieve this and more, we must always pull the plug of the world at the end of the day and plug it into the heart of God.

Hear from Him, allow Him to direct you, and your life will be transformed daily to the glory of the Kingdom of God.

**Confession:** My life is an example used by God to show His will to the world. I am not negatively influenced by the world, and I only do the will of God. My ears are fixed on the heart of God, and what He says becomes true in my life.

**Prayer:** Lord Jesus, I ask for the grace to return to your presence. I ask for the grace to come to your throne of mercy to cleanse my heart daily. I pray that my lifestyle pleases you daily and the stain of the devil does not mar me forever. Amen.

# DAY THIRTEEN:

## LIFE TO THE BODY, SOUL, AND SPIRIT

*Bible verse: 'And if Christ is in you, the body is dead because of sin, but the Spirit is life because of righteousness. But if the Spirit of Him who raised Jesus from the dead dwells in you, He who raised Christ from the dead will also give life to your mortal bodies through His Spirit who dwells in you,'* Romans 8:10-11.

Have you taken some time to explore the Bible in search of the power of God? Have you taken the time to read the word of God to see the things that Jesus Christ did here on earth through the power of God in Him? Have you taken note of the lives that were touched, changed, and turned around? Do you know that with God by your side and in you, there is really nothing like death? Let us take a short look at the encounter with Lazarus. John 11:38-44 says, *'Then Jesus, again groaning in Himself, came to the tomb. It was a cave, and a stone lay against it. Jesus said, "Take away the stone." Martha, the sister of him who was dead, said to Him, "Lord, by this time there is a stench, for he has been dead four days." Jesus said to her, "Did I not say to you that if you would believe you would see the glory of God?" Then they took away the stone from the place where the dead man was lying. And Jesus lifted up His eyes and said, "Father, I thank You that You have heard Me. And I know that You always hear Me, but because of the people who are standing by I said this, that they may believe that You sent Me." Now when He had said these things, He cried with a loud voice, "Lazarus, come forth!"* And *he who had died came out bound hand and foot with graveclothes, and his face was wrapped with a cloth. Jesus said to them, "Loose him, and let him go."*

Lazarus was dead for days and decaying in the tomb, yet he was raised up again. Jesus Christ is interested in you, and he is also interested in giving life to you and all that concerns you. There is nothing we ask in Faith that is too big or too small for God to do.

Also, we must remember that God is never late. It just is not time for that miracle to come yet if you truly believe. When we call on the name of Jesus, our voices are heard. We are His and He is ours, and so are our problems. The miracle performed in the life of Lazarus is one of the many miracles that Jesus performed and is also not the height of what he can do. For a start, you are alive today and reading this despite all that you have been through. With a consistent life in Christ, you will be spending all of eternity in the Kingdom of God. These amongst others should let us know that we are loved. The power of God in us gives us life and resurrects everything that feels dead in us. Whatever you may encounter in your body, soul, or spirit, take it to God! Take it to His feet and ask Him to take control of the situation.

Just like Lazarus, I pray for you today that everything that feels dead in you begins to come alive. Amen.

**Confession:** I walk in the miracles of the hand of the Lord. My life is evidence of His mercies and kindness, and every dry bone in my life begins to rise again.

**Prayer:** I thank you, God, for your hand in my life. Thank you for breathing life into me, and for being involved in my day-to-day. I pray that your resurrection power stays with me and in me. I pray that anything that is currently experiencing death in my life is put under the power of your grace and mercy. Amen.

Dr. Brenda Jefferson

# DAY FOURTEEN:

## AS FAR AS YOUR FAITH GOES

***Bible verse:*** *'So Jesus answered and said to them, "Have faith in God. For assuredly, I say to you, whoever says to this mountain, 'Be removed and be cast into the sea,' and does not doubt in his heart, but believes that those things he says will be done, he will have whatever he says. Therefore I say to you, whatever things you ask when you pray, believe that you receive them, and you will have them,'* Mark 11:22-24.


A short statement I live by to date is this: God will only work as far and as much as I give Him the chance to. He is an all-knowing God that always wants the best for us, but He will not invade our lives and make us do things that He knows are best for us. I learned this the hard way when I would get into some kind of trouble, and I would stamp my feet on the ground and ask God why He let me do that thing. I learned that God has given us the freedom to live our lives as we please, but also a choice to live it the way He wants us to, in the way that brings glory to His name.

We all have various different desires in our hearts, and we have certain areas of our lives that we need God to show up in, and of course, God can do it all. The question is 'is your faith grounded enough to carry that?'

The woman with the issue of blood had such great faith that she did not need any confirmation from anyone. She did not need to ask any questions, she did not need anyone to hold her hands as she walked towards Jesus, and she did not even need Jesus to be in a healing mood or healing other people so she could join the queue. In faith, she said to herself 'If only I can touch the hem of his garment, I know I will be made whole.' It is not news to us that she really was made whole.

The wife of the dead prophet who was in debt is another example of the extent to which our faith can go. 2 Kings 4:1-7 says, *'A certain woman of the wives of the sons of the prophets cried out to Elisha, saying, "Your servant my husband is dead, and you know that your servant feared the Lord. And the creditor is coming to take my two sons to be his slaves." So Elisha said to her, "What shall I do for you? Tell me, what do you have in the house?" And she said, "Your maidservant has nothing in the house but a jar of oil." Then he said, "Go, borrow vessels from everywhere, from all your neighbors — empty vessels; do not gather just a few. And when you have come in, you shall shut the door behind you and your sons; then pour it into all those vessels, and set aside the full ones." So she went from him and shut the door behind her and her sons, who brought the vessels to her; and she poured it out. Now it came to pass, when the vessels were full, that she said to her son, "Bring me another vessel." And he said to her, "There is not another vessel." So the oil ceased. Then she came and told the man of God. And he said, "Go, sell the oil and pay your debt; and you and your sons live on the rest."*

Two things we can get from this - 1. Our faith is our saving grace. 2. The extent of one's faith is the extent of their miracle. We can see that the oil did not stop flowing until there were no more jars to take it. So, if this widow got 50 jars, they would have all been filled up. If she got a hundred or a thousand, those too would have been filled up. But she got as much as she thought was enough, as far as her faith could reach.

So, how far does your faith in the power of God go?

**Confession:** My faith will move mountains - mountains of pain, mountains of disdain, mountains of lack and poverty, and every other undesirable mountain in my life. I am powerful in Christ Jesus because of my faith. Hallelujah!

**Prayer:** Jesus, I have seen the way that you move in the lives of people. I have seen the power that comes from believing in you and I want that too. I pray for the strengthening of my faith in you so that I never belittle your power in my life. Amen.

# DAY FIFTEEN:

## THE PROMISES OF GOD AGAINST THE LIES OF THE WORLD

**Bible verse:** *'I beseech you therefore, brethren, by the mercies of God, that you present your bodies a living sacrifice, holy, acceptable to God, which is your reasonable service. And do not be conformed to this world, but be transformed by the renewing of your mind, that you may prove what is that good and acceptable and perfect will of God,'* Romans 12:1-2.

If you have not heard it enough, I come to tell you this today. The devil is working full-time to ensure that he frustrates you out of the presence of God and out of the beautiful life that God has planned for you. He wants you mad, tired, angry, bitter, and confused, and whatever he needs to do to achieve that, I assure you that he would do it ten times over and some more. A major way that the devil has attacked Christians of this age and time is by getting into their thoughts. The Bible says in Romans 12:2 that we should not conform to this world and its ways but we should renew out minds with the word and will of God.

The popular saying goes; As a man thinks, so is he. What do you think this may mean? It means that what you think of yourself is where actually you place yourself. If you think that you are forsaken, then you will be forsaken. If you think that you are broken, poor, weak, and destroyed, then you are right! However, if you think and know in your heart that you are blessed, then your mind will attract all the goodness of the Lord and the blessings will be yours.

The devil knows this and that is why he works full-time to do one thing: change your thought patterns.

Maybe you committed a sin against God some days ago and you feel very bad about it. On top of that guilt, the devil will add shame to it and say to us 'you are too unclean to go before the throne of God the Father.' However, the Bible says in 1 John 1:9, *'If we confess our sins, He is faithful and just to forgive us our sins and to cleanse us from all unrighteousness.'* The devil will whisper in your ears that you would die from a life-threatening disease, in pain and poverty, whereas, God says in His word *'Bless the Lord, O my soul, and forget not all His benefits: Who forgives all your iniquities, who heals all your diseases, who redeems your life from destruction, who crowns you with lovingkindness and tender mercies, who satisfies your mouth with good things, so that your youth is renewed like the eagle's.'* (Psalm 103: 2-5) The devil will also say to you that salvation is not yours because your sins and that of your ancestors are yours to bear but the sacrifice made by Jesus on the cross tells us otherwise.

So, ask yourself the big question today: whose word am I going with? Are you going to allow the lies of the devil to poison your thoughts and give you an undesirable reality? Or are you going to feed your body, soul, and spirit with the truth in the Word of God and allow your life to turn around for good? Whose voice will you listen to regarding your future? What decision will you make?

**Confession:** The devil has nothing on me. My life is a testimony to the glory of God, and this will never be stolen from me. My mind works as the Lord made it to, never in sync with the thoughts of the devil. I am blessed and highly favored!

**Prayer:** My God and King, I know you have given me the power to shape my life in the way that I want. I thank you for making it possible for my life to be as glorious as you will. Thank you for giving me leverage over the devices and plots of the wicked one. I pray that this remains forever, and whatever the devil has in store for me be rebuked in the name of Jesus, Amen.

Dr. Brenda Jefferson

# DAY SIXTEEN:

## GET THEE BEHIND ME, SATAN

***Bible verse:*** *'I am the door. If anyone enters by Me, he will be saved, and will go in and out and find pasture. 10 The thief does not come except to steal, and to kill, and to destroy. I have come that they may have life, and that they may have it more abundantly,'* John 10:9-10.

Again, the devil is working full-time to pull down as many Christians as he can. The bible tells us in 1 Peter 5:8 that the devil is actually moving around seeking who to devour. He is not resting for one bit, all he wants is to pull you and I down and far away from the arms of God.

Matthew 16:21-23 says, *'From that time Jesus began to show to His disciples that He must go to Jerusalem, and suffer many things from the elders and chief priests and scribes, and be killed, and be raised the third day. Then Peter took Him aside and began to rebuke Him, saying, "Far be it from You, Lord; this shall not happen to You!" But He turned and said to Peter, "Get behind Me, Satan! You are an offense to Me, for you are not mindful of the things of God, but the things of men."* Jesus looked at Peter and called him 'Satan' because Peter was speaking against the word and will of God.

What can we see in this?

1. The enemy is closer than you think. Anyone around you can be used by God and the same person can also be used by the devil, as long as they allow it to happen.
2. You must be watchful at all times. The devil wants to kill, steal and destroy, and he will come when you least expect it. You must have a vigilant spirit to cut out his advances and stay true and in line with the will of God.
3. Cut him at the door. If the devil comes visiting, do not wait for him to come in before you ask him to leave. You must send him back at the door before he utters any more words. You must take a strong stance to shun him and tell him to get behind you. This way, you show that you are not gullible or open to his advances toward you.

No matter what he says, do not listen to him. Your situation now does not directly define who God is. It also does not define who you are, so be careful to filter out the noise that the devil makes and bring your ears close to the heart of God.

**Confession:** The devil has no say in my life. The will of God is final and that is the path that my life will follow. I refuse to give ear to his lies, and I command him to flee from me now and forever more.

**Prayer:** Help me to shun the devil and all of the moves he tries to make. Lord, please give me the grace, strength, and wisdom that I need to lock him out and place my focus on you. Amen.

Dr. Brenda Jefferson

# DAY SEVENTEEN:

## BEHOLD THE FACE OF GOD

***Bible verse:*** *'But you, Israel, are My servant, Jacob whom I have chosen, the descendants of Abraham My friend. You whom I have taken from the ends of the earth, and called from its farthest regions, and said to you, 'You are My servant,*

*I have chosen you and have not cast you away: Fear not, for I am with you; be not dismayed, for I am your God. I will strengthen you, yes, I will help you, I will uphold you with My righteous right hand,'* Isaiah 41:8-10.

In the world today, many Christians have a constant misunderstanding of who God really is. We see Him as a big, tall, and stern judge who seats up there and decides who gets sent to hell and who comes into His kingdom in heaven. We typically think that the moment we sin, He is utterly disappointed in us, and He turns His back on us but this is untrue. We think this way because we are so focused on our sins, our shortcomings, and our wrongs that we take our face away from the Lord and the sacrifice He made for those sins. This idea we have affects the way we relate with Him, which in turn, affects our spirituality and our prayer lives.

The story of the prodigal son should tell us how accepted and loved we are by God. We know we have done wrong, but this does not mean we are condemned forever. After asking for forgiveness of sin, we need to look up to the face of God to see the approval on it.

God still loves you and I, no matter the gravity of our mistakes and errors.

If we spend time eating the Word of God, all of our doubts will be met with the promises and covenants that God has made over us. We will then be reminded that the Lord is invested in our prosperity and blessings. God wants to help you, bless you, and fix you. Are you ready to accept all of these?

Now, when we look unto God, we become transformed into His image. This was the case with Moses after he spent so much time with God. Exodus 30:29-30 says, *'Now it was so, when Moses came down from Mount Sinai (and the two tablets of the Testimony were in Moses' hand when he came down from the mountain), that Moses did not know that the skin of his face shone while he talked with Him. So when Aaron and all the children of Israel saw Moses, behold, the skin of his face shone, and they were afraid to come near him.'* He had spent so much time in the presence of God that he started to shine in the glory of God.

The glory of the Lord will rub off on you when you spend time looking unto Him. And likewise, if you spend time looking at the world and its ways, that will also rub off on you.

God is calling you today to turn to Him in every stage of your life, be it good, bad, or ugly. His arms are open and waiting for you to run into them.

**Confession:** I am created in the image of God. My thoughts are of God, my words are of God, and my actions are of God too. I am a child of God, living and breathing in His goodness. Amen.

**Prayer:** You are kind and merciful to me always, Lord. You have granted me the chance to be more like you in my dealings of life. You have given me the opportunity to come to you any day and anytime. I thank you for this in Jesus' name, Amen.

# DAY EIGHTEEN:

## A THANKFUL HEART

***Bible verse:*** *'Make a joyful shout to the Lord, all you lands! Serve the Lord with gladness; come before His presence with singing. Know that the Lord, He is God; It is He who has made us, and not we ourselves; We are His people and the sheep of His pasture. Enter into His gates with thanksgiving, and into His courts with praise. Be thankful to Him, and bless His name. For the Lord is good; His mercy is everlasting, and His truth endures to all generations,'* Psalms 100:1-5.

Thanksgiving is not always easy or direct. Sometimes, we tend to think 'I am thankful and grateful all the time' but the exact opposite is what it really is because we do not pay enough attention to it. But being thankful to God is something we must do for His will to come to pass in our lives. Being thankful gives glory to God and His Kingdom, but it also does something very significant for us; it allows us to move from the level of faith we are at to higher realms of faith both for ourselves and for the people around us.

Being thankful allows for joy to rest in our hearts and in our spirits. The devil and his angels are enemies of our faith, and they will do anything they have to do to steal our joy. The devil does not want you happy, and he does not want you thankful either. When we give thanks to God, especially when we are in difficult life situations, we render the enemy a loser in a very important battle in our lives.

Giving thanks to God in tight or tough situations please God and causes Him to move on His throne. When you put yourself in a position of constant praise and thanksgiving, you take away access to your life from the devil, because really, he can never operate while you are joyful, thankful, and grateful. God is always looking for such a Christian, one who holds on to his praise no matter what.

In short, being thankful in down times is considered a sacrifice to God. It is you telling Him 'this may not be where I want to be right now, but I can see that you are working, so thank you.'

There is great power in a heart that is thankful, and that power does great work in the life of such a person.

Being thankful brings a feeling of contentment. Rather than focusing on all that is wrong, being thankful magnifies the seemingly little right things that are working for you. When you are not thankful, you will find so many reasons to worry and be sad, and this will dry up your soul. Many people have it worse, but a heart that is not thankful will only focus on those who have it better. Being thankful is trusting in the timing of God and following in the steps of Jesus. He knew death was waiting for Him, but He never stopped giving thanks.

Are you thankful for where you are in life right now? Do you recognize the love of God in His gift of life and the gift of His Son for your salvation?

You must always practice praise because it can and will turn your situation around while making your heart happy and light.

**Confession:** I see beyond my situation in life, and I am thankful for where I am at. I refuse to focus on the bad. I choose to trust God to move me ahead, but I am thankful every day for His works in me. Amen.

**Prayer:** Father in Heaven, please forgive me for the many times that I have not been grateful enough to you. Forgive me for focusing on the bad things when you have blessed me with so much more riches. I ask that you help me to fix my heart so I may be thankful to you. Amen.

Dr. Brenda Jefferson

# DAY NINETEEN:

## A LAMP TO MY FEET

***Bible verse:*** *'All Scripture is given by inspiration of God, and is profitable for doctrine, for reproof, for correction, for instruction in righteousness, that the man of God may be complete, thoroughly equipped for every good work,'* 2 Timothy 3:16.

There was once a young man who wanted a new television set in his home. He had one that was no longer serving its purpose and he wanted to get rid of it. He also wanted something very special, pretty, and unique. So, he walked into a mart and began his search. After spending hours looking for something that sparked his interest, he finally saw an unusual-looking television set in a shop. He walked in, asked a few questions, and was convinced that was what he wanted and needed. The set was a very new model and only a few people had gotten their hands on it. The seller was explaining a few features, but this man was caught up with its beauty and soon, he paid for it and took it home.

He set it up after many long hours and proceeded to turn it on. He used it for a long time the same way he used his old television set until the day his little nephew came around and showed him all that the television could do to make his life better at home. After hearing it all, this man sat on his couch, wondering how much easier his life would have been if only he knew more about the television and all that it was made to do.

As Christians, we must know one thing for a fact - the power in the word of God can turn our lives around if we take the time to study. John 1:1-5 says, *'In the beginning was the Word, and the Word was with God, and the Word was God. He was in the beginning with God. All things were made through Him, and without Him, nothing was made that was made. In Him was life, and the life was the light of men. And the light shines in the darkness, and the darkness did not comprehend it.'* When we hold the Bible in our hands, we hold the power to turn our lives around. The little story up there would have been completely different if the man in question did one thing; if he read the manual that came with the set. The manual is a letter from the manufacturer to the user, telling them everything they need to know to enjoy the product to the fullest capacity. Likewise, the Bible is a manual for living, a letter from the creator of life to us, telling us how to navigate through life to get the very best out of it.

Ignoring the Bible is telling God that you can do without his help, and this is both untrue and unwise. The Bible blesses our lives from our insides. We must see it as daily food that we must eat to be revitalized so that we can face life head-on.

We have been equipped with all that we need to live life to the fullest in the way intended by God. Whether we do or do not do this is completely our decision to make.

Dr. Brenda Jefferson

**Confession:** I declare that without Christ, I am nothing. I spend time daily acquiring wisdom at the feet of the Lord, and this will put me a step ahead for the rest of my life.

**Prayer:** Thank you for giving me the gift of your Word, Heavenly Father. Thank you for caring for my well-being enough to give me your Word to guide me and lead me right. By the power in the name of Jesus, I come against every power that will make me feel fulfilled or satisfied without your input in my life. Amen.

# DAY TWENTY:

## WORKING TOWARD THE SAME GOAL

***Bible verse:*** *'Therefore, my beloved, as you have always obeyed, not as in my presence only, but now much more in my absence, work out your own salvation with fear and trembling; for it is God who works in you both to will and to do for His good pleasure,'* Philippians 2:12-13.

No matter how troubling life gets, our one most important goal must always remain to spend eternity in the bosom of the Lord when the time comes. I know that life gets hard, and we get so occupied with trying to right the wrongs and fix everything we lay our hands on. But truly, that is not the true essence of life.

We have been called to be Sons of God. That is the goal we must always work toward, and not get so knee-deep in fixing our lives on earthly matters. The Bible says in John 10:11, *'I am the good shepherd. The good shepherd gives His life for the sheep.'* and really, it does make me relax a bit and want to just drop all I am doing to run into the hands of Jesus.

What does it mean to be a shepherd? The sole work of a shepherd is to care for his sheep, and Jesus tells us that this is who He is. It worries me that we have a great and powerful 'caretaker' who is so invested in keeping us safe, providing for us, and keeping us satisfied, but we choose to take that into our hands and abandon our own primary assignment.

1 Thessalonians 5:11 says, *'Therefore comfort each other and edify one another, just as you also are doing.'* We are all heading towards the same goal. Rather than pursue riches and all things that the world offers, we can hold each other's hands and run towards our eternal race.

We do not want to spend our time on earth doing all the wrong things, only to regret it later and search for a second time.

Your problems are heavy now, but the Lord wants to take it up and have you work on your heart and your salvation. This is your sole assignment.

**Confession:** I have my eyes fixed on the Lord and the assignment that has been given to me. I am not carried away by my problems, and I do not choose to solve my issues by myself. I have a God who cares for me and will sort my issues.

**Prayer:** Thank you for your word, Lord Jesus. I do not want to spend my life on what is not necessary. Please, help me stay fixed on your will and assignment for me. Help me live a life that pleases you always. Amen.

# Seasons

Dr. Brenda Jefferson

# PART THREE: TRUST IN GOD

## DAY TWENTY-ONE:

### BY HIS STRIPES, WE ARE HEALED.

***Bible verse:*** *'Who Himself bore our sins in His own body on the tree, that we, having died to sins, might live for righteousness—by whose stripes you were healed,'* 1 Peter 2:24.

Now, we know what Passover means and what it signifies. How can this information be useful to us and our bodies?

During the celebration of Passover, Jesus broke bread and handed it to His disciples saying, 'this is my body which is given for you'. We may or may not know this, but do we know what it signifies? Jesus knew that in the hours following the Passover, the flesh of the Lamb of God (himself) would be beaten, torn, crucified, bruised, spat on, and eventually buried. He knew that for our sake and the sake of our bodies, His own body would be broken apart for one big reason: so your own body will not have to break.

What does this say to us? Why did Jesus have to break bread and also pass round wine which signified the blood of the Lamb meant for salvation and protection from harm and death? The answer is quite simple: God is extremely interested in healing our bodies, just as he is interested in our salvation. Every whip that Christ received was for our sake, to combat illness, to combat cancer, disease, and infirmity. It was to overcome the hold of terminal disease and to give life to us so when we go through all of these, we must know that it is not ours to bear! Give it to Jesus. Let Him in today. The lie the devil tells us is that God is more interested in the state of our hearts than our bodies and our health, but does one not affect the other? Does your physical and mental wellness not affect your relationship with God?

This is the simple truth about what God wants for us. When you are in doubt, remember this! When the devil tells you to sit with the pain that you feel, or that it is 'human' to fall sick and feel daunting pain, remember this. Nothing is too human for God to be involved in. He created you, and he cares for you. He cares for your health, he wants to heal you of every disease and pain, and he wants you to live a fulfilling life. Keep this in mind always.

By partaking in communion regularly, you remind God of the covenant that has been made and sealed. You let him know that you should feel no pain in your body because Jesus Christ has felt all the pain on your behalf, and you remind yourself of your place as a child of God.

**Confession:** I am healed. I have the strength of Christ in me. I have strong bones, I have good blood flowing in my veins, and I will live a long, good life on earth. Amen.

**Prayer:** Thank you for your love, Lord Jesus. Thank you for settling my health and wellness thousands of years ago, and making sure that I have a safe place in you. Thank you for healing my scars and my wounds. I pray today for the wisdom to turn to you at all times, and to look unto your face in my down moments. I accept that for my sake, Christ carried sickness, sorrow, pain, torment, disease, and fear. I, therefore, receive the grace to be free from all of these things. In Jesus' name.

Amen.

# DAY TWENTY-TWO:

## NOT BY BREAD ALONE

***Bible verse:*** *'Then Jesus was led up by the Spirit into the wilderness to be tempted by the devil. And when He had fasted forty days and forty nights, afterward He was hungry. Now when the tempter came to Him, he said, "If You are the Son of God, command that these stones become bread." But He answered and said, "It is written, 'Man shall not live by bread alone, but by every word that proceeds from the mouth of God,'* Matthew 4:1-4.

We have been told over many years that we need food to survive. We need to eat breakfast, lunch, and dinner to survive and give our bodies the nutrients that it needs to function properly, but the Bible and the life of Jesus on earth tell us otherwise. In Matthew chapter 3, Jesus was baptized and a voice from heaven said 'this is my beloved Son, in whom I am well pleased'. This is to assure us that everything that followed after the baptism in the life of Jesus Christ was clearly not a result of his own actions or inactions, and so, it was not a punishment from God. Jesus was then led by the Spirit into the wilderness to be tempted by the devil. This was no small feat, and Jesus knew that, so He prepared His body and His Spirit by doing two things: Fasting and Praying. Jesus began His weighty and extremely important ministry by fasting, and that was how He also overcame the enemy.

Many Christians wonder why fasting is so important or even necessary in their growth. The answer is that fasting helps you to rely more on God and on His power than on the things of life and the things that the eyes can see. For every time that we decide to give food a break and focus on God, we say to Him, 'God, not by bread alone, not by the world alone, not by my needs alone, but by your power and by your being.'

We don't need food to survive (this does not cancel out the importance, of course). We need the word of God, and because the word of God is God Himself, then we need God to survive. We need to eat the Word of God like we will eat food daily, and live by its principles. When the world is standing by what it thinks is best, you choose to stand by what God says is best for you. Your life is unique and tangible to God, and His being is just as important to our existence.

We need to dwell on the truth in the word of God on a daily basis and hold on to it for dear life. The Bible says in Hebrews 4:12-13, *'For the word of God is living and powerful, and sharper than any two-edged sword, piercing even to the division of soul and spirit, and of joints and marrow, and is a discerner of the thoughts and intents of the heart. And there is no creature hidden from His sight, but all things are naked and open to the eyes of Him to whom we must give account.'* The power is just what we need to cope in life and we have been given unlimited access. May we have the wisdom to use it in the right way.

**Prayer:** Thank you for the power in your word that gives life, Lord Jesus. Thank you for giving me unending access to the gift of healing and the fullness of life in you. Amen.

**Confession:** I have all the life I need in Christ alone. My hope and my strength are in God, and I do not lack the vitality that I need to live life well.

Dr. Brenda Jefferson

## DAY TWENTY-THREE:

## YOU ARE BEING PREPARED FOR GREATER THINGS

***Bible verse:*** *'The preparations of the heart belong to man, but the answer of the tongue is from the Lord. All the ways of a man are pure in his own eyes, but the Lord weighs the spirits. Commit your works to the Lord, and your thoughts will be established,'* Proverbs 16:1-3.

In the life that we live here on earth, we must always remember that we are created by a God who cares about us and wants us to live in the best ways, the way that he intended for us. We have not been created and abandoned here on earth to figure out our ways. God watches over us and places a longing in our hearts, in line with the destiny He has planned for us. The big question is: Do you trust Him enough to hold on to His Word, His judgments, and the plans He has for you?

The plans that God has for each of us, are not free of rough slides. Of course, all things that come from the Lord are good and right, but no one says it is going to be easy. The Bible lets us know a couple of times that when the going gets tough, God is going to be with us all the way, it did not say we would have it all handed to us on a platter. Nothing that is worth having is ever going to come to you without some kind of opposition and difficulty. The storms in the sea will come, and we will have our fears reignited and confronted, but it is in all of these that we gain important skills and learn lessons that push us further ahead into the plans of God for us.

So, why does God allow for those paths to be difficult? Why does He sit up there in Heaven and allow us to go through certain things that come as opposition? The answer is clear: He is making you. The position you are in right now has the power to determine what you are and what you can become, to a very large extent. If you live with a family where curfew or lights out is strictly 9pm, it grows on you, and you become adept at that. Likewise, our situations in life allow us to grow as we find a way to deal with them. During the experience you have with your difficulties, you will come to see that you are dropping undesirable attributes and picking up ones that will eventually get you very far. God is very intentional about your growth, and He will do just about anything to see you move from where you are now to where He wants you to be, both physically, spiritually, morally, intellectually, and in every other way that there is.

When I sit to think about certain things in my life and why they are not exactly going the way I want, I tell myself this, God loves me too much to give me an uplift or promotion that I am not ready for.

Following God's lead is the best thing we can do for our future, our sanity and peace of mind, and our growth. As we follow Him, we will be forced to make hard decisions that will most often seem unnatural and inhumane, but that is indicative of the spirituality of that decision. We make choices that distinguish us and quickly put our flesh to death, spiritual death which means submission to the superiority of the spirit.

God is preparing a place of glory for you and for me, and until the last days when we see Jesus Christ face to face, His direction, lead, and guidance are all that we need to take us far enough into His plans for us.

**Confession:** I am a dedicated follower of Christ. All my hope is in the Lord, and He does not lead me into wrong places. He guides and leads me right, all the days of my life.

**Prayer:** Lord Jesus, thank you for thinking of me. Thank you for sorting my future, even long before I was born. I ask for the grace and wisdom to plant my feet in your own footsteps. Open the eyes of my heart to see you more. In Jesus' name, Amen.

# DAY TWENTY-FOUR:

## INSIDE OUT

**Bible verse:** *'Now to Him who is able to do exceedingly abundantly above all that we ask or think, according to the power that works in us, to Him be glory in the church by Christ Jesus to all generations, forever and ever. Amen,'* Ephesians 3:20.

In the jungle or forest, we see lions birthing cubs that eventually become lions too, and we see reptiles of different kinds produce offspring, each of their kind. The moment a reptile births a cub, there is a big problem of imbalance, and this is unlikely to happen, and vice versa! The reason is glaring; you will only be able to give off from what is in you.

We have been granted grace in many different ways, and God says that He is willing to do more in us, many more than we could ever think of or ever ask for, if only we allow Him to work in us. The level to which we allow him to work determines the level of greatness that we will see happening from our insides. To move further ahead into the plans that God has for us, we just have to let him have his way. It may seem rough and tough, not as we envision, but it is what is good for us. Some relationships, dreams, and marriages are dropped off and abandoned because rather than give way to the will and word of God, we give way to the weakness of the flesh.

Today, make up your mind that your dreams will not die in the 'oven.' Every stage of life that you find yourself in is an opportunity to give in to the authority of the Spirit of God. It is an opportunity to learn the lesson attached to that stage because God is very intentional and never lets anything just happen. You must learn to trust that God is handling your situation in the most loving way. He is with you all the way, guiding you safely. Daily, your task should be to understand the moves of God at that point. Understand what He wants to instill into you, and take due time to soak it in. You can either choose to lean on Him and not be entitled to 'your life' and 'your rules', or you can choose to be the king of your own life and face whatever the consequences may look like.

*So, what is your decision today?*

**Confessions:** Every day, I grow bigger and better. The hand of God is evident in my life and who I was yesterday is not better than who I am today. I am evolving and growing to become the man/woman intended by God.

**Prayer:** Lord, please work in me. Help me to overcome every single thing in my life that may pose an obstacle to your flow in my life. Put me in a position that is constantly ready to receive from you now and forever more. Amen.

# DAY TWENTY-FIVE:

## WHERE THE SPIRIT OF THE LORD IS

**Bible verse:** *'Now the Lord is the Spirit; and where the Spirit of the Lord is, there is liberty,'* 2 Corinthians 3:17.

Does anyone that is reading this really understand what bondage is or what it can feel like? If you have ever been held in a place against your wish for some time, maybe you could recall how that felt. Maybe you could also recall being made to do something that you really do not want to do, but you have no choice because you are under 'bondage' and so, you are made to do those things. Do you know how that feels?

Now, this is exactly how an addiction would feel too! In many stages of addiction, the victim knows that the endpoint of that action is bad and leads to no good for them. They know they should not be doing that thing, like smoking that cigarette or igniting fires that lead to immorality, but they just seem stuck, almost like they have to do that thing to move on.

That right there is what we call bondage.

After sin got into the world because of the actions of the first Adam and his partner, Eve, sin got the power to put people in bondage. This is because the bloodline of man became corrupt so sin could hold the children of God in bondage, making them do things that they know they should not be doing.

God looked down on us and felt pity for the human race. Mind you, this bondage of sin does not come with just sin. It also comes with all the possible impurities you can think of; illness or sickness, disease, death, poverty, pain, sorrow, and many more. God did not want these for his children. He wanted freedom, so He gave us Himself and His Son, Jesus Christ.

After the sacrifice, the battle was won and now, you and I have true freedom from all that the devil tries to do against us. We have freedom in that we can flee sin, we can overcome temptations, we can pray to our God and get answers, and we can live a life pleasing to God.

You are no longer a slave to sin. It is no longer considered normal for a man to fall for the temptations of the devil, to get terribly ill and die of that sickness. All of those are in the past.

It may seem impossible for you to let go of that addiction, but with God, all things are possible, and we have been granted freedom, as long as we come into His presence.

This verse also lets us know that we now have access to freely come into the presence of God. It is no longer how it used to be in the past times when priests would walk into the temple backward to hear from God and then relay the message to the people, no! Now, there is freedom, freedom from slavery, freedom from sin, freedom from addiction, freedom from pain and sorrows, and freedom from any other thing we can think of that holds us down against our wishes. This is so because the price for all of these things has been paid for in full by the sacrifice Jesus made on the Cross of Cavalry. He fought the battle against all, and He won!

As long as you have the Spirit of God living in you, and you have established a close relationship with God, then you are a partaker of this freedom. Live it!

**Confession:** I am free from bondage. I am no longer a slave to sin, so I am not constantly pushed to displease God. My mind is cleansed, and my body is made to please the Lord for the rest of its days.

**Prayer:** Lord Jesus, thank you for your sacrifice of love. Thank you for freeing me from eternal bondage. Thank you for giving me power over a life that does not please you or give me any gain. I pray that this is never stolen away by the devil and that I have the wisdom to make use of my freedom to your glory. In Jesus' name, I pray, Amen.

Dr. Brenda Jefferson

# DAY TWENTY-SIX:

## GREATER IS HE

***Bible verse:*** *'For whatever is born of God overcomes the world. And this is the victory that has overcome the world — our faith. Who is he who overcomes the world, but he who believes that Jesus is the Son of God?'* 1 John 5:4-5.

Throughout the Bible, we see a few other references that tell us one very important message - that every man who believes in Christ has Him living inside him. That is, as long as a person has announced their faith and denounced their disbelief in God, then Christ lives in them. The message we would like to touch on is the effect this living has on the life of the believer. In a few words, this living gives strength to the believer. We are told that He who lives in us is far greater than the entire world. He is greater than our troubles, greater than sickness, greater than pain, and even greater than death as He fought this and won when He was crucified. This is a reminder that we are never alone in anything we do or are faced with. It is a guarantee that simply because I believe in God, I can no longer be taken down or torn apart by the uncertainties of life. This is an assurance that we do not have to be afraid of anything or worry about anything, but we should always practice peace in our hearts because we have been sorted.

To have Christ living in our bodies, in the temple that we have prepared to be holy and fit for Him to live in, means that we have overcome all of our worries, concern, and troubles!

As a child of God, you do not have to be afraid or have the same worry as those who do not believe in the sovereignty of Christ. As a child is to a father, you are His responsibility.

Ephesians 3:16-19 says, *'that He would grant you, according to the riches of His glory, to be strengthened with might through His Spirit in the inner man, that Christ may dwell in your hearts through faith; that you, being rooted and grounded in love, may be able to comprehend with all the saints what is the width and length and depth and height — to know the love of Christ which passes knowledge; that you may be filled with all the fullness of God.'* For this home to be made in your heart by Jesus, you have to trust in Him completely. You have to live a life that he endorses, one that pleases Him. The scripture says very constantly that Jesus will live within you when He has a place in you.

It does not matter the lie that the devil tries to feed you, be it about your health, the longevity of your life, your prosperity, or anything at all. None of it will matter because you have the truth within you, unshaken and undiluted.

God is always near you and He will never take Himself out of your life. Always remember this when you are faced with difficult situations. God is involved in your well-being. He resides in you and cares for all that concerns you.

**Confession:** I am more than a conqueror. My life is a testimony of victory over the devil, and it stays that way. I am a testimony of the power of God.

**Prayer:** Lord, thank you for being a good and loving Father to me, for having mercy and compassion over me, and for caring for all that concerns me. Thank you for giving me victory over the world by dwelling in me. Today, I ask for the strength to continue this battle. I ask that you uphold me when I become weary and give me the grace to keep you in my heart. Amen.

# DAY TWENTY-SEVEN:

## REST IN HIS POWER

***Bible verse:*** *'So the Lord said to him, "What is that in your hand?" He said, "A rod." And He said, "Cast it on the ground." So he cast it on the ground, and it became a serpent; and Moses fled from it,'* Exodus 4:2-3.

God has not, for once, left us by ourselves. In the Old Testament, Moses was about to be given a very important task that would allow for the children of God to be released from slavery in Egypt. A point worthy of note is that Moses was a stammerer, so imagine his shock when he was told that he was about to be sent on an assignment to Pharoah. God knew that before he came to Moses, of course, but God does not look at the stature of a man before He chooses to use them. He looks at the insides, what the man is made of from within.

Look within yourself today, beyond your fears, beyond your worries, beyond your inadequacies, and beyond your physical qualities. What do you think you have in your hand? It must not be anything extra or something huge and magnificent. For Moses, it was just a rod and it was transformed into a snake right in his eyes. For little David the shepherd, it was five stones and a sling, and with this and the blessing of God, he was able to bring down the mighty giant, Goliath. For Jesus, it was five loaves and two fishes, and with the blessing of God, it fed a great multitude of people and there were many leftovers gathered afterward.

Whatever you have with you is more than enough when it is brought before the Lord for blessing. The question is, are you willing to trust the Lord today with that little you have so it can yield even far more than you can imagine? Is your trust in the Lord and do you believe in his transforming power?

What you have is enough to bring glory to God. You are enough to bring glory to God. God can use you, no matter what. He can lift you up from the nothing that you see to the great person you hope to become.

You are enough by every means possible. You are not too slow, too ill, too daft, too poor, too young, or too small to do a great thing. Remember, He that is in you is far greater than he that is in the world. Jesus is stretching out his hand to you today, asking you to trust Him with the little in your hand and listen to His instructions to watch that thing multiply to bless you and those around you very richly. Are you ready to trust Him with what is in your hand and do as He tells you to?

**Confession:** God has blessed my hands and He has given me all that I need to return glory to Him. I walk in wisdom, power, and strength to use my gift to the lifting of the Kingdom of God here on earth. Amen.

**Prayer:** I know that all you have given to me is good and able to lift me from where I am to where you have set for me. I ask for your help in finding out what these things are. I also ask for the grace to

## Seasons

discern them in good time, so that I can fall in place, and position myself for the blessings you have for me. Amen.

Dr. Brenda Jefferson

# DAY TWENTY-EIGHT:

## POWERHOUSE OF FAITH

*Bible verse:* *'By faith, Enoch was taken away so that he did not see death, "and was not found, because God had taken him"; for before he was taken he had this testimony, that he pleased God. But without faith, it is impossible to please Him, for he who comes to God must believe that He is and that He is a rewarder of those who diligently seek Him,'* Hebrews 11:5-6.

Each time I think of faith and what it means to me as a Christian, I see it as some sort of great gift, or leverage that is given to as many as they are that believe in the power of God. Faith, as the Bible says, is just like an easy way of pleasing God and without it, we are unable to please Him. One may ask, why is this? How important is faith that I cannot please God without it, even with good works and loving my neighbor? The answer is this: if truly you are a Christian, then faith is the foundation of your lifestyle. What does this mean?

To a man who has no faith, anything he does not see or know for a fact is not true because it has no grounds to stand by. If he did not see it happen, or have some factual reference, then it is unreal. To this same man, the sacrifice made on the Cross of Cavalry for the sake of all sinners born and unborn is just not real and does not make sense in any way.

I mean, how can a Spirit come from Heaven to earth, only to die for the sake of sinners, and simply because someone born two thousand years later believes in this, then he is saved from a bloodline of sin? How would that sound to a man without faith? It will sound absurd.

However, we have faith in the sacrifice of love that was made on our behalf, and it is that faith that makes us who we are in Christ; sons and daughters of righteousness.

Faith is a weapon given to each of us to successfully navigate through life. We see in Hebrews 11 what faith was able to do for men and women alike. Verses 7-11 say:

*'By faith Noah, being divinely warned of things not yet seen, moved with godly fear, prepared an ark for the saving of his household, by which he condemned the world and became heir of the righteousness which is according to faith. By faith, Abraham obeyed when he was called to go out to the place which he would receive as an inheritance. And he went out, not knowing where he was going. By faith he dwelt in the land of promise as in a foreign country, dwelling in tents with Isaac and Jacob, the heirs with him of the same promise; for he waited for the city which has foundations, whose builder and maker is God. By faith, Sarah herself also received the strength to conceive seed, and she bore a child when she was past the age because she judged Him faithful who had promised.'*

Faith places us one step ahead as children of God. It 'sorts' us and attends to our fears and worries. It gives us a spirit of calmness when those who do not believe hassle their way through. Truly, our faith will be tested over time, but we must keep returning to the presence of God to renew this by eating the word daily and announcing our places as heirs of the throne of Grace.

**Confession:** My faith is my stronghold to God and His promises to me. My faith is renewed daily, and I have no doubt in me that it will push me further to please God with my life. Amen.

**Prayer:** I may lose everything I have in life, but I never want to lose my faith in you, Lord. I want my trust in you to grow daily as I live so that the troubles of life do not get the better of me. Help me in this, I pray. Amen.

# DAY TWENTY-NINE:

## PATIENCE AND INTENTIONAL LIVING

***Bible verse:*** *'Do not be deceived, God is not mocked; for whatever a man sows, that he will also reap. For he who sows to his flesh will of the flesh reap corruption, but he who sows to the Spirit will of the Spirit reap everlasting life. And let us not grow weary while doing good, for in due season we shall reap if we do not lose heart,'* Galatians 6:7-9.

Patience is not just a likeable trait that we should have as humans. It is a character that the Lord encourages us to build, and of course, for our own good. A part of the Bible I would love to point toward is James 5:1-11. It reads, 'Therefore be patient, brethren, until the coming of the Lord. See how the farmer waits for the precious fruit of the earth, waiting patiently for it until it receives the early and latter rain. You also be patient. Establish your hearts, for the coming of the Lord is at hand. Do not grumble against one another, brethren, lest you be condemned. Behold, the Judge is standing at the door! My brethren, take the prophets, who spoke in the name of the Lord, as an example of suffering and patience. Indeed, we count them blessed who endure. You have heard of the perseverance of Job and seen the end intended by the Lord—that the Lord is very compassionate and merciful.'

Many times, we forget that everything is not in our control, no matter how hard we work. If it takes 10 years for a mango tree to bear fruit, planting ten trees in one year will not give you the mango fruit in one year. These things can never be manipulated.

God is a God of process, and during those 10 years, a lot of things will fall in place.

This is to encourage you to not waste time trying to fix what is out of your control. After you have done all that you can do, the next step to take is to be patient. Be careful, so you do not rush your learning process and make a mess of everything.

While it is easy to get scared and worried about the output, we must also have hope in the power of God to fix our lives, so it is smooth and desirable. Also, please remember that you were not created for this world so you must live with eternity at the top of your priority continually. Let God be your guide and stay the course. Let us pray.

**Confession:** I have the patience that I need to fully trust in the Lord. I refuse to impatiently expect results. While my testimony is coming, I am learning and growing, just as the Lord pleases.

**Prayer:** Lord, I ask for the grace to live patiently. I want to trust in you and reap the result of patience. I want to hear from you and know when to move and when to stop. Grant me this, In Jesus' name. Amen.

## DAY THIRTY:

### HOPE IN GOD

***Bible verse:*** *'For I know the thoughts that I think toward you, says the Lord, thoughts of peace and not of evil, to give you a future and a hope. Then you will call upon Me and go and pray to Me, and I will listen to you. And you will seek Me and find Me, when you search for Me with all your heart,'* Jeremiah 29:11-13.

Having hope is a belief that a good thing is going to happen or come to you. Hope is present when you are in a situation, and you convince yourself that there is more to come, and your situation is not the end of the story for you. It is convincing yourself that though the storm is here, there will be calm, and a silver lining will appear on the cloud. It is telling yourself that things are dark and gloomy at the moment, but joy will come in the morning. Looking at these instances, we can imagine how empowering hope can be, just like fuel to fire. God is asking us to have hope in Him, not in the system of the country, not in the doctor's reports, not in the paycheck at the end of the month, but in Him and His unwavering love.

He is calling out to you today that you have faith in Him once more. Faith in the plans He has for you and faith in who He has been since the beginning of time.

It does not get amazingly easy and because God knows this, He has blessed us with the Holy Spirit to lead us and comfort us.

Each time you feel an emptiness in your heart, look unto God and ask for help to stay strong. This is because, in the end, He is all that matters. Everything else will pass away, and He is the only one that will stand true to us.

Spend your life investing in this, and you will never be made to regret it.

**Confession:** No matter what life brings my way; I will continually put my hope in God. I will not turn away from His face, and I will not lose faith in His word over me.

**Prayer:** Faithful Father, I thank you because you are just and true, and your love for me never fails. I know it can and will get hard at some point, so I ask that you give me the power to stay in line with your will, trusting you all the way. Amen.

# Seasons

## NOTES:

## ABOUT THE AUTHOR

**DR. BRENDA JEFFERSON** is essential to the body of Christ. Her passion for the Word of God, gospel music, worship, and her creative ability to write, allows her to inspire others in a positive way. She is a bright light in the lives of many, embarking for change and calling others toward Holiness. Through the mission and ministry of her husband, Bishop M.B. Jefferson, she is Co-Pastor of Living in Victory Christian Church, Deeper Life Christian Church, and World Assemblies Fellowship International. She also helps to oversee The House of David Help Center and is CEO of Scripture Music Group.

With ministry at the forefront of her heart, she is submissive to the call of God on her life. Together, they work diligently to release strongholds, unite relationships, deliver those bound from addiction, empower the youth, and be a united influence for Jesus. In these uncertain times of pandemic, poverty, wars, and famine, she is necessary for this generation. Her 'last days' message of repentance, faith, and good works captivates the masses. Through truth and humility, she is devoted to her assignment and seeks to help those in need.

# Seasons

Dr. Brenda Jefferson

## OTHER WORKS BY AUTHOR

PRAISE HIM WHILE YOU WAIT

RHEMA THROUGH MY SONG

TRIUMPH THROUGH PAIN

## MUSIC & ALBUMS

A TIME OF REFRESHING

TRIUMPH THROUGH PAIN

SUPERNATURAL

INVOCATION

*You Tube Channel:* Dr. Brenda Jefferson

*Instagram:* DrBrendaJ

www.brendajefferson.com

www.livcc.org

www.ingramcontent.com/pod-product-compliance
Lightning Source LLC
Chambersburg PA
CBHW041142110526
44590CB00027B/4097